26

Religion in
Public Schools

Religion in Public Schools

Alan Marzilli

SERIES CONSULTING EDITOR
Alan Marzilli, M.A., J.D.

CHELSEA HOUSE
PUBLISHERS
A Haights Cross Communications Company

Philadelphia

CHELSEA HOUSE PUBLISHERS

VP, New Product Development   Sally Cheney
Director of Production   Kim Shinners
Creative Manager   Takeshi Takahashi
Manufacturing Manager   Diann Grasse

Staff for RELIGION IN PUBLIC SCHOOLS

Editor   Patrick M.N. Stone
Production Assistant   Megan Emery
Photo Editor   Sarah Bloom
Series and Cover Designer   Keith Trego
Layout   21st Century Publishing and Communications, Inc.

A Haights Cross Communications ✈ Company

http://www.chelseahouse.com

First Printing

1 3 5 7 9 8 6 4 2

Library of Congress Cataloging-in-Publication Data

Marzilli, Alan.
  Religion in public schools / by Alan Marzilli.
     p. cm. -- (Point/counterpoint)
Includes index.
Contents: Religion in public schools: historical roots and current
controversies -- Prayer should be allowed to return to public schools -
- Prayer does not belong in public classrooms -- Religious clubs in
public schools should be treated more fairly -- Religious clubs in
public schools have unfair advantages -- Schools should teach
alternatives to evolution -- Schools should treat evolution as
definitive -- Religion in public schools: a look to the future.
  ISBN 0-7910-7484-6
  1. Religion in the public schools--United States--Juvenile
literature. [1. Religion in the public schools. 2. Church and state.]
I. Title. II.
Series: Point-counterpoint (Philadelphia, Pa.)
  LC111.M325 2003
  379.2'8'0973--dc21

                                           2003009544

CONTENTS

Introduction
Alan Marzilli, M.A., J.D.
Durham, North Carolina

The debates presented in POINT/COUNTERPOINT are among the most interesting and controversial in contemporary American society, but studying them is more than an academic activity. They affect every citizen; they are the issues that today's leaders debate and tomorrow's will decide. The reader may one day play a central role in resolving them.

Why study both sides of the debate? It's possible that the reader will not yet have formed any opinion at all on the subject of this volume—but this is unlikely. It is more likely that the reader will already hold an opinion, probably a strong one, and very probably one formed without full exposure to the arguments of the other side. It is rare to hear an argument presented in a balanced way, and it is easy to form an opinion on too little information; these books will help to fill in the informational gaps that can never be avoided. More important, though, is the practical function of the series: Skillful argumentation requires a thorough knowledge of *both* sides—though there are seldom only two, and only by knowing what an opponent is likely to assert can one form an articulate response.

Perhaps more important is that listening to the other side sometimes helps one to see an opponent's arguments in a more human way. For example, Sister Helen Prejean, one of the nation's most visible opponents of capital punishment, has been deeply affected by her interactions with the families of murder victims. Seeing the families' grief and pain, she understands much better why people support the death penalty, and she is able to carry out her advocacy with a greater sensitivity to the needs and beliefs of those who do not agree with her. Her relativism, in turn, lends credibility to her work. Dismissing the other side of the argument as totally without merit can be too easy—it is far more useful to understand the nature of the controversy and the reasons *why* the issue defies resolution.

The most controversial issues of all are often those that center on a constitutional right. The Bill of Rights—the first ten amendments to the U.S. Constitution—spells out some of the most fundamental rights that distinguish the governmental system of the United States from those that allow fewer (or other) freedoms. But the sparsely worded document is open to interpretation, and clauses of only a few words are often at the heart of national debates. The Bill of Rights was meant to protect individual liberties; but the needs of some individuals clash with those of society as a whole, and when this happens someone has to decide where to draw the line. Thus the Constitution becomes a battleground between the rights of individuals to do as they please and the responsibility of the government to protect its citizens. The First Amendment's guarantee of "freedom of speech," for example, leads to a number of difficult questions. Some forms of expression, such as burning an American flag, lead to public outrage—but nevertheless are said to be protected by the First Amendment. Other types of expression that most people find objectionable, such as sexually explicit material involving children, are not protected because they are considered harmful. The question is not only where to draw the line, but how to do this without infringing on the personal liberties on which the United States was built.

The Bill of Rights raises many other questions about individual rights and the societal "good." Is a prayer before a high school football game an "establishment of religion" prohibited by the First Amendment? Does the Second Amendment's promise of "the right to bear arms" include concealed handguns? Is stopping and frisking someone standing on a corner known to be frequented by drug dealers a form of "unreasonable search and seizure" in violation of the Fourth Amendment? Although the nine-member U.S. Supreme Court has the ultimate authority in interpreting the Constitution, its answers do not always satisfy the public. When a group of nine people—sometimes by a five-to-four vote—makes a decision that affects the lives of hundreds of millions, public outcry can be expected. And the composition of the Court does change over time, so even a landmark decision is not guaranteed to stand forever. The limits of constitutional protection are always in flux.

These issues make headlines, divide courts, and decide elections. They are the questions most worthy of national debate, and this series aims to cover them as thoroughly as possible. Each volume sets out some of the key arguments surrounding a particular issue, even some views that most people consider extreme or radical—but presents a balanced perspective on the issue. Excerpts from the relevant laws and judicial opinions and references to central concepts, source material, and advocacy groups help the reader to explore the issues even further and to read "the letter of the law" just as the legislatures and the courts have established it.

It may seem that some debates—such as those over capital punishment and abortion, debates with a strong moral component—will never be resolved. But American history offers numerous examples of controversies that once seemed insurmountable but now are effectively settled, even if only on the surface. Abolitionists met with widespread resistance to their efforts to end slavery, and the controversy over that issue threatened to cleave the nation in two; but today public debate over the merits of slavery would be unthinkable, though racial inequalities still plague the nation. Similarly unthinkable at one time was suffrage for women and minorities, but this is now a matter of course. Distributing information about contraception once was a crime. Societies change, and attitudes change, and new questions of social justice are raised constantly while the old ones fade into irrelevancy.

Whatever the root of the controversy, the books in POINT/ COUNTERPOINT seek to explain to the reader the origins of the debate, the current state of the law, and the arguments on both sides. The goal of the series is to inform the reader about the issues facing not only American politicians, but all of the nation's citizens, and to encourage the reader to become more actively involved in resolving these debates, as a voter, a concerned citizen, a journalist, an activist, or an elected official. Democracy is based on education, and every voice counts—so every opinion must be an informed one.

The search for religious freedom was one of the driving forces behind the colonization of America and the formation of the United States. However, just as religion is an extremely personal matter, Americans define "religious freedom" in many different ways. Since the early 1960s, when the Supreme Court held that organized school prayer violates the Constitution, the public schools have been a battleground for students, parents, teachers, politicians, and lawyers fighting over the role of religion.

Many people want the freedom to read the Bible, pray in school, and share religious teachings with classmates. But others want to attend a public school completely free from interference with the religious beliefs learned at home or in houses of worship. Some want to suppress topics—such as evolution or sex education—that conflict with their religious beliefs. This book examines both sides of controversial issues such as school prayer, religious clubs, and the teaching of evolution.

Religion in Public Schools: Historical Roots and Current Controversies

Since the colonial era, religious freedom has been a central concept in American government. However, throughout the years, government officials, religious leaders, and everyday citizens have debated the meaning of religious freedom. The controversy began when settlers of the various colonies—many of whom had faced religious persecution in Britain and other countries of their origin, countries with established official churches—responded differently to the persecution that they had faced:

> [L]ike the Puritans of the Massachusetts Bay Colony, they erected theocracies and persecuted those of divergent belief; or, like the settlers of Rhode Island, they realized that the essence of religious freedom and integrity was religious liberty for everyone.[1]

After the American Revolution, the Constitution strongly supported the idea of religious freedom, but left its definition rather vague. The First Amendment to the U.S. Constitution states, "Congress shall make no law respecting an establishment of religion, or prohibiting the free exercise thereof. . . ." Like many important clauses in the Constitution, the establishment clause and the free exercise clause are sparsely worded. As a result of the lack of any lengthy explanation, these clauses have been subject to widely varying interpretations by the courts.

Religion and the U.S. Constitution

• **How different would the United States be if only people of a certain religion were allowed to vote?**

In addition to being somewhat vague, these two clauses concerning religious freedom in America sometimes seem to be in conflict with one another. By enacting a policy that protects an individual's right to freely exercise one's own religious practices, the government might appear to be endorsing religion. Similarly, policies that are designed to limit the influence of religion in the public sphere might infringe upon people's right to exercise religion freely. Many have suggested that the only way to balance the two is to erect a "wall of separation between church and state"—that the government should remain neutral on religious matters.

On the other hand, the Constitution makes no mention of this "wall of separation," and many critics contend that religion has long had an important place in American government, from presidential inauguration speeches, to prayers in classrooms nationwide. For nearly two centuries after the enactment of the First Amendment, many Americans took for granted these types of religious expression, considering them both acceptable and constitutional.

In 1952, the Supreme Court had held that public schools could release students during the school day for religious instruction or worship outside of school.[2] However, as immigration and societal change made the country more diverse, the influence of religion in the public schools began to come under fire.

> • **Where does the phrase "separation of church and state" appear in the Constitution? What does it really mean?**

Landmark Cases Involving School Prayer

In 1958, Steven Engel visited his children's New York elementary school and was shocked to see that his children were praying in a way that conflicted with the family's Jewish religion. He recalled:

> I saw one of my children with his hands clasped and his head bent. . . . After, I asked him, "What were you doing?" He said, "I was saying my prayers." I said, "That's not the way we say prayers."[3]

In Baltimore, Madalyn Murray O'Hair had a similar reaction upon discovering children praying when she enrolled her son in a public school:

> It was just a few moments after 9:00 A.M. and pupils were in their homerooms. Suddenly, a swell of young voices engulfed us. As we passed one open classroom door after another, we heard the recitation, in unison, of the Lord's Prayer. . . .
> I turned to Bill. "My gawd, what was that?"
> Of course, I "knew" but I was really testing my sanity.[4]

O'Hair's objection was, however, on slightly different religious

It was Madalyn Murray O'Hair, the founder of American Atheists, who began the landmark case of *Murray* v. *Curlett* (1963), which banned organized prayer in public schools. O'Hair, shown here in 1963 with sons William (left) and Jon Garth, quickly became one of the most controversial figures in American politics. She remained an outspoken atheist until 1995, when she, along with her son Jon and William's daughter Robin, was kidnapped and murdered by an employee of the American Atheists office. William Murray converted to Christianity in 1980 and is a practicing evangelist today.

grounds. She was an atheist, and because she denied the existence of God, she believed that it was improper for public schools to encourage students to pray.

> • **What should be done when a student has religious objections to subjects taught in a science class? What about student objections to material taught in a history class?**

At the time, the experiences of Steven Engel and Madalyn Murray O'Hair were by no means unusual. Throughout the nation, public school teachers led their classrooms in prayer, sometimes in accordance with the students' religious upbringings and sometimes not. Accordingly, because these parents and others like them decided to challenge the widespread practice of school prayer, the U.S. Supreme Court decided to examine the issue.

In a landmark decision, the Supreme Court sided with Engel's view that his children should not be praying in public schools. In *Engel* v. *Vitale*,[5] (1962) the Court ruled that New York's practice of leading children in a "nondenominational" prayer composed by the State Board of Regents violated the establishment clause of the Constitution. Soon after, the Court ruled in *Abington School District* v. *Schempp*[6] (1963) that Baltimore schools could not lead students in the Lord's Prayer, and that reading Bible verses in public school also violated the establishment clause. Some saw these decisions as victories for religious freedom, but others saw them as attacks upon religion itself.

The Legacy of the School-Prayer Cases

In the years that followed, it was somewhat difficult to determine which activities would violate the Constitution and which would not. In the landmark *Lemon* v. *Kurtzman* decision (1971), the Court spelled out three tests that are used to determine whether a government action violates the establishment clause of the Constitution:

> First, the statute must have a secular legislative purpose; second, its principal or primary effect must be one that

neither advances nor inhibits religion, . . . [and] finally, the statute must not foster "an excessive government entanglement with religion."[7]

Often, the "Lemon test" is applied by asking whether the state would appear to be endorsing religion by taking a particular action.

Application of the Lemon test has resulted in the acceptance of certain seemingly religious activities by state governments and their subdivisions—such as public school systems. Still, the Supreme Court has remained steadfast against the practice of leading classrooms or student gatherings in prayer. For example, in *Lee* v. *Weisman* (1992),[8] the Court struck down the practice of a member of the clergy leading a nondenominational prayer at a high school graduation. And in *Santa Fe Independent School District* v. *Doe* (2000),[9] the Court held that prayers could not be broadcast over the public address system at high school football games.

Many people have attacked the Supreme Court's establishment clause jurisprudence, noting that the phrase "separation of church and state" does not appear in the Constitution. Attorney Peter J. Ferrara has argued that the establishment clause simply prohibits discrimination—for or against a particular religion, or for or against religion in general:

> The no-discrimination doctrine would allow substantially greater prayer and Bible reading in the public schools. The state could still not author a prayer and mandate its use nor mandate the recital of a particular prayer from one religion, like the Lord's Prayer. . . . [However, a] policy of starting the day with the teacher choosing, on a rotating basis, a volunteer student to make or read a statement of some fundamental moral lesson . . . which could be a prayer or a passage from the Bible . . . would be acceptable.[10]

Despite angry claims nationwide that the Supreme Court has "kicked God out of the public schools," there remains a great deal of religious activity—both legal and illegal—in public schools today. Despite clear pronouncements by the Supreme Court, many schools continue to lead their students in prayer; each year cases make headlines when students or their parents protest. At the same time, some have called for an amendment to the Constitution that would allow prayer in public schools.

The most common form of religious activity in public schools today is participation in religious clubs, such as Bible study clubs. Although the federal Equal Access Act and several Supreme Court cases have upheld the operation of voluntary

FROM THE BENCH

Public Schools May Release Students for Religious Worship

From *Zorach* v. *Clauson*, 343 U.S. 306 (1952):

The First Amendment . . . does not say that in every and all respects there shall be a separation of Church and State. Rather, it studiously defines the manner, the specific ways, in which there shall be no concert or union or dependency one on the other. That is the common sense of the matter. Otherwise the state and religion would be aliens to each other—hostile, suspicious, and even unfriendly. Churches could not be required to pay even property taxes. Municipalities would not be permitted to render police or fire protection to religious groups. Policemen who helped parishioners into their places of worship would violate the Constitution. . . .

We would have to press the concept of separation of Church and State to these extremes to condemn the present law on constitutional grounds. The nullification of this law would have wide and profound effects. A Catholic student applies to his teacher for permission to leave the school during hours on a Holy Day of Obligation to attend a mass. A Jewish student asks his teacher for permission to be excused for Yom Kippur. A Protestant wants the afternoon off for a family baptismal ceremony. In each case the teacher requires parental consent in writing. In each case the teacher, in order to make sure the student is not a truant, goes further and requires a report from the priest, the rabbi, or the minister. The teacher in other words cooperates in a religious program to the extent of making it possible for her students to participate in it. Whether she does it occasionally for a few students, regularly for one, or pursuant to a religious clubs in public schools, many people who believe in a strong separation of church and state worry that schools are too supportive of the clubs, whether by endorsing the clubs' messages, providing financial support, or allowing them to detract from classroom instruction.

- **Which makes more sense — a "no-discrimination doctrine" or a "separation of church and state"?**

Debates also arise when people with strongly held religious beliefs object to certain parts of a school's curriculum. A common

systematized program designed to further the religious needs of all the students does not alter the character of the act.

We are a religious people whose institutions presuppose a Supreme Being. We guarantee the freedom to worship as one chooses. We make room for as wide a variety of beliefs and creeds as the spiritual needs of man deem necessary. We sponsor an attitude on the part of government that shows no partiality to any one group and that lets each flourish according to the zeal of its adherents and the appeal of its dogma. When the state encourages religious instruction or cooperates with religious authorities by adjusting the schedule of public events to sectarian needs, it follows the best of our traditions. For it then respects the religious nature of our people and accommodates the public service to their spiritual needs. To hold that it may not would be to find in the Constitution a requirement that the government show a callous indifference to religious groups. That would be preferable to those who believe in no religion over those who do believe. Government may not finance religious groups nor undertake religious instruction nor blend secular and sectarian education nor use secular institutions to force one or some religion on any person. But we find no constitutional requirement which makes it necessary for the government to be hostile toward religion and to throw its weight against efforts to widen the effective scope of religious influence. The government must be neutral when it comes to competition between sects. It may not thrust any sect on any person. It may not make a religious observance compulsory. It may not coerce anyone to attend church, to observe a religious holiday, or to take religious instruction. But it can close its doors or suspend its operations as to those who want to repair to their religious sanctuary for worship or instruction. No more than that is undertaken here.

In the mid- to late nineteenth century, as Catholic immigrants flooded into the United States and met with strong anti-Catholic sentiment, the debate over the Bible's place in public schools became volcanic. It was assumed that religion was the basis of education; public funds often went to Protestant schools but never to Catholic schools, which were considered "sectarian" and exclusive. Protestant texts and prayers became a part of the standard curriculum. In reaction, the growing Catholic population lobbied for a total removal of Protestant teachings and began to form parochial schools. This nineteenth-century political cartoon illustrates the enormity of "nativist" anti-Catholic sentiment: Catholic Irish immigrants are depicted as enemies of the "nonsectarian" Protestant public school curriculum.

example today can be found in objections to sex education; many religious groups have pushed for "abstinence only" curricula. Yet, the most notable example of religious objections to curriculum material is probably the objection to the teaching of Darwinian evolution theory, which conflicts with the biblical account of creation in the Book of Genesis. The issue took center stage during the famous "Scopes Monkey Trial" of 1925, in which a Tennessee schoolteacher was fined for teaching evolution—many citizens accused evolutionists of blasphemy for teaching that humans evolved from monkeys. Today, attacks on evolution continue, as proponents of theories consistent with the biblical story of creation attempt to influence state educational standards.

Not surprisingly, debates over the extent of religious activity frequently cause not only local controversy, but also capture national attention. Groups like the American Civil Liberties Union (ACLU) and People for the American Way often side with parents who believe that they—not the public schools—should be responsible for their children's religious upbringing. Taking the other side are groups such as the American Center for Law and Justice, which has argued before the Supreme Court for the expanded role of religion in public schools. Because both the practice of religion and freedom of religion are central to American life, the battle over religion in the public schools will continue to rage, from small towns to Washington, D.C.

Since the colonial era, both religion and religious liberty have been of utmost importance to American law and society. The values imparted by these beliefs are reflected in the Constitution, which guarantees freedom of religion and prohibits the establishment of an official religion. The debate over the role of religion in the public schools began in earnest in the 1960s, when the Supreme Court ruled that organized classroom prayer was unconstitutional.

Prayer Should Be Allowed to Return to Public Schools

In recent years, school-prayer supporters have suggested amending the U.S. Constitution to allow prayer to return to public schools and other aspects of public life. Yet, many people believe that the legitimacy of school prayer is not contingent on the passage of such an amendment. To them, the framers of the Constitution never intended a "wall of separation between church and state," and therefore, school prayer is an activity that is legitimate under the current Constitution. Many believe that the Supreme Court was wrong when it decided in 1962 that a nondenominational prayer composed by the New York Board of Regents was "wholly inconsistent" with the U.S. Constitution.[1] Before 1962, school prayer was common, being deeply ingrained in the American heritage.

• **Does prayer belong in public schools?**

Supporters of school prayer believe that it is not only legal, but sorely needed in order to restore American values to young people and rescue a failing educational system. Nationally there is widespread support for school prayer, with some areas of the country being more ardent supporters of the idea than other regions. In fact, in many places, school prayer has continued despite the Supreme Court's pronouncements. As court cases pop up on occasion, many people resent the fact that the Supreme Court and lower courts constantly thwart the will of educators, parents, and students in their efforts to initiate (or keep) prayer in public schools.

Prayer is a vital part of the American heritage.

School-prayer advocates firmly believe that nothing in the U.S. Constitution prohibits prayer in public schools. The First Amendment to the Constitution begins, "Congress shall make no law respecting an establishment of religion." For nearly two centuries after the enactment of the Bill of Rights (the first ten amendments), prayer was as much a common feature in public schools as it was in many facets of public life.

During the colonial period, many colonists had fled religious persecution in Britain and other nations. The English monarchy had established the Church of England as the official church, and members of other denominations were not allowed to practice their religion openly. Individual colonies had been settled by large numbers of people of one religion or another—Quakers, Catholics, and other denominations—and some colonies had even established official religions. However, the framers of the Constitution saw a strong federal government as a threat, and therefore sought to prohibit the federal government from establishing an official church.

Still, despite prohibitions on establishing any particular church, religion remained important in the private lives of American citizens, and being a government "of the people, for the people," in American governmental affairs as well. Coins

September 13, 1954: Public schools in Washington are integrated for the first time, and students join in prayer. Even in the tumultuous years of the early civil rights movement, when integration was causing enormous political upheaval, prayer in public schools was still the norm. This would remain the case until the early 1960s.

carried the motto, "In God We Trust," and sessions of the state legislatures, Congress, and the Supreme Court opened sessions with prayers. In an effort not to elevate any particular religion over another, most of these prayers were "nondenominational," meaning that they were designed to be acceptable to people from a wide range of Judeo-Christian religions. For example, the U.S Supreme Court opened with the invocation, "God save the United States and this Honorable Court."[2]

After the Civil War, the "Reconstruction Amendments" were passed in an effort to make former slaves full citizens of the nation. Among these amendments was the Fourteenth Amendment, which reads in part, "No state . . . shall deprive any person of life, liberty, or property without due process of law. . . ." In the latter half of the twentieth century, the Supreme Court began to interpret the Fourteenth Amendment as meaning that the Bill of Rights applied to the states as well as to Congress. Under this reasoning, the states—like Congress—would be prohibited from establishing a religion. The development of this type of jurisprudence set the stage for a court battle over school prayer.

> • **Has American society changed since colonial times? Has the meaning of the U.S. Constitution changed? Enough? Too much?**

When *Engel* v. *Vitale* came before the Court, school prayer was widely accepted. In the words of Justice William O. Douglas, the state and federal government was "honeycombed" with funding and support of non-denominational religious activity. Just a few years earlier, in 1954, Congress had added the words "under God" to the Pledge of Allegiance, which was recited each day by schoolchildren nationwide. Nevertheless, the Court struck down prayer in public schools, holding:

> There can be no doubt that New York's state prayer program officially establishes the religious beliefs embodied in the Regents' prayer. . . . Neither the fact that the prayer may be denominationally neutral nor the fact that its observance on the part of the students is voluntary can serve to free it from the limitations of the Establishment Clause . . . . When the power, prestige and financial support of government is placed behind a particular religious belief, the indirect coercive pressure upon religious minorities to conform to the prevailing officially approved religion is plain.[3]

To many observers, the Court's decision in the case marked a radical departure from establishment clause jurisprudence. Most Supreme Court decisions—although they involve new legal questions—are based in large part on the "precedent" established by prior Supreme Court decisions. A typical Supreme Court case makes reference to past decisions in deciding the question at hand. But in a break from established practice, the six-justice majority did not cite a single previous decision of the Court that supported its conclusion that the establishment clause prohibits nondenominational prayer in public schools.

FROM THE BENCH

Was *Engel* Wrongly Decided?

From *Engel* v. *Vitale*, 370 U.S. 421 (1962)
(Stewart, J., dissenting):

It might ... be argued that parents who want their children exposed to religious influences can adequately fulfill that wish off school property and outside school time. With all its surface persuasiveness, however, this argument seriously misconceives the basic constitutional justification for permitting the exercises at issue in these cases. For a compulsory state educational system so structures a child's life that if religious exercises are held to be an impermissible activity in schools, religion is placed at an artificial and state-created disadvantage.... And a refusal to permit religious exercises thus is seen, not as the realization of state neutrality, but rather as the establishment of a religion of secularism, or at the least, as government support of the beliefs of those who think that religious exercises should be conducted only in private....

Our decisions make clear that there is no constitutional bar to the use of government property for religious purposes. On the contrary, this Court has consistently held that the discriminatory barring of religious groups from public property is itself a violation of First and Fourteenth Amendment guarantees....

The dangers both to government and to religion inherent in official support of instruction in the tenets of various religious sects are absent in the present cases, which involve only a reading from the Bible unaccompanied by comments which might otherwise constitute instruction. Indeed, since, from all that appears in

> • **Is it the role of the Supreme Court to protect the rights of the minority against the will of the majority?**

Critics of the decision have accused the Supreme Court of "legislating politics from the bench," removing the power to make important decisions from the hands of the people and the legislatures and transferring that power to a group of nine judges who meet behind closed doors. In the words of Robert Bork, whose 1987 nomination to the Supreme Court was rejected by the Senate:

either record, any teacher who does not wish to do so is free not to participate, it cannot even be contended that some infinitesimal part of the salaries paid by the State are made contingent upon the performance of a religious function.

In the absence of evidence that the legislature or school board intended to prohibit local schools from substituting a different set of readings where parents requested such a change, we should not assume that the provisions before us — as actually administered — may not be construed simply as authorizing religious exercises, nor that the designations may not be treated simply as indications of the promulgating body's view as to the community's preference.... In the *Schempp* case there is evidence which indicates that variations were in fact permitted by the very school there involved, and that further variations were not introduced only because of the absence of requests from parents. And in the *Murray* case the Baltimore rule itself contains a provision permitting another version of the Bible to be substituted for the King James version.

It is clear that the dangers of coercion involved in the holding of religious exercises in a schoolroom differ qualitatively from those presented by the use of similar exercises or affirmations in ceremonies attended by adults. Even as to children, however, the duty laid upon government in connection with religious exercises in the public schools is that of refraining from so structuring the school environment as to put any kind of pressure on a child to participate in those exercises; it is not that of providing an atmosphere in which children are kept scrupulously insulated from any awareness that some of their fellows may want to open the school day with prayer, or of the fact that there exist in our pluralistic society differences of religious belief.

The Court headed by Chief Justice Earl Warren from 1953 to 1969 occupies a unique place in American law. It stands first and alone as a legislator of policy, whether the document it purported to apply was the Constitution or a statute.[4]

Bork writes that the Supreme Court's application of the establishment clause to the states, "prohibit[ing] religious practices that the states had employed for many years . . . has done much to alter the moral tone of communities across the country."[5]

Although the *Engel* case involved a prayer written by the New York Board of Regents, it soon became clear that any form of school-sponsored prayer was unacceptable. The following year, in *Abington School Dist.* v. *Schempp* (1963),[6] the Supreme Court struck down a Pennsylvania law requiring that school days begin with a reading of Bible verses and a Maryland law requiring the reading of the Bible or the recitation of the Lord's Prayer. The *Engel* and *Schempp* decisions sent shock waves through the nation, and many vowed not to comply with the ban on school prayer.

> • **Should people disobey the Supreme Court's decisions if they disagree with them?**

In New York, where the *Engel* case originated, the Engel family and other plaintiffs were subjected to threats, harassment, and vandalism. The Catholic archbishop of New York City lashed out at the Court's decision:

> I am shocked and frightened that the Supreme Court has declared unconstitutional a simple and voluntary declaration of belief in God by public school children. The decision strikes at the very heart of the Godly tradition in which America's children have for so long been raised.[7]

Many school-prayer advocates continue to believe that the Supreme Court's interpretation of the establishment clause in *Engel* and subsequent cases was incorrect, and that school boards and educators should act upon their consciences and support school prayer regardless of the state of the law. In 2002, 40 years after the *Engel* decision, a school in Indiana remained intent on having the school choir sing the Lord's Prayer at graduation ceremonies, despite a lawsuit brought by the parents of twins who sang in the choir. According to the magazine *Church & State*:

> Officials at the school had been advised by their attorney to drop the Christian prayer but voted to include it anyway. Randall Pryor, the school board president, declared that the prayer would stay in because "we are Christians" and said, "lawyers be damned."[8]

Other school-prayer supporters, realizing that the Supreme Court's reading of the establishment clause is firmly entrenched in American law, have advocated for an amendment to the Constitution that would specifically authorize prayer in public schools. Representative Ernest Istook (R-Oklahoma) introduced "an amendment to the Constitution of the United States restoring religious freedom," which reads in part: "the people's right to pray and to recognize their religious beliefs, heritage, and traditions on public property, including schools, shall not be infringed." Proponents of prayer in public schools argue that school prayer has educational benefits and reflects the will of the majority.

The absence of prayer harms public schools.

Many people agree that our nation's public schools are facing a great crisis, with low test scores, violence, pregnancies, and suicides among the many problems plaguing the public school system. Some school-prayer advocates have blamed the removal of prayer from public schools for many of these problems. For example, David Barton, president of Wallbuilders, in Aledo, Texas, writes:

> [W]hen the Courts ruled that students might not use the Ten Commandments, nor study the Scriptures, nor learn about sexual abstinence, etc., the separation of these teachings caused personal, individual harm to those students.[9]

Barton's book, *America: To Pray or Not to Pray*, suggests that public education and health have been on the decline since 1963, an effect attributable to the ban on school prayer in that year's *Schempp* decision. Using statistics compiled from various government sources, his charts show a marked increase in sexually transmitted diseases, teen pregnancies, alcohol consumption, and violent crime, as well as a marked decrease in SAT scores, all beginning in 1963. He also points to a moral decline since the decisions, which he characterized by increases in premarital sex, cohabitation, and divorce rates.

Supreme Court Justice Antonin Scalia, who has been critical of the Court's decisions concerning religion, pointed out that nondenominational prayers serve the very practical function of bringing together people of different religions, thereby reducing religious discrimination. Dissenting in *Lee* v. *Weisman*, which held that a public school could not invite a member of the clergy to deliver a prayer at graduation, Justice Scalia wrote:

> [T]he Founders of our Republic knew the fearsome potential of sectarian religious belief to generate civil dissension and civil strife. And they also knew that nothing, absolutely nothing, is so inclined to foster among religious believers of various faiths a toleration—no, an affection—for one another than voluntarily joining in prayer together, to the God whom they all worship and seek. Needless to say, no one should be compelled to do that, but it is a shame to deprive our public culture of the opportunity, and indeed

the encouragement, for people to do it voluntarily. The Baptist or Catholic who heard and joined in the simple and inspiring prayers of Rabbi Gutterman on this official and patriotic occasion was inoculated from religious bigotry and prejudice in a manner that cannot be replicated. . . . Going to the extreme of banning non-denominational prayer actually has the unintended effect of advancing religious discrimination.[10]

> • **To what extent can society's problems be blamed on the ban on school prayer?**

Many parents and students support prayer in school.

Many school-prayer advocates believe that the Supreme Court has essentially thwarted the will of the people by outlawing prayer in schools. Not only was public support for prayer in schools strong at the time of the *Engel* decision, but it remains strong today. In reaction to a 2002 ruling by a federal court in California that the words "under God" rendered the Pledge of Allegiance unconstitutional—a decision that has been sharply criticized and not put into effect—an ABCnews.com poll revealed that 89 percent of Americans support the Pledge of Allegiance as it stands.[11]

Throughout the nation, there continue to be incidents in which students, parents, and educators are firmly behind school prayer, but reacting to complaints from a single person or a handful of people, a federal judge prevents a school from doing what the remainder of the community strongly supports.

In 2002, such an incident occurred in West Virginia. St. Alban's High School had planned to have a school prayer said at the graduation ceremony, just as it always had. However, one of the graduating seniors happened to be an atheist. After he persuaded a federal judge to issue an order blocking prayer at the graduation ceremony, the community reacted strongly to the judge's order. School principal Tom Williams told the press that the prayer "was something the kids wanted," and according to the Charisma News Service:

> [The] seniors heeded the biblical admonition to always pray and not give up. . . . [They] didn't allow an atheist classmate and a federal judge to spoil their graduation ceremony Thursday night. Defying a court order blocking a school-sanctioned invocation, more than 100 students stood, bowed their heads and recited the Lord's Prayer.[12]

After the students rose in prayer, the audience gave the students a standing ovation.

> • **Is there a difference between students joining together to lead a prayer and a school board or principal telling students to pray?**

Stories like this one in West Virginia are unfortunately all too common, according to school-prayer advocates. Polls indicate that a wide majority of Americans support school prayer in opposition to the Supreme Court's decisions. In 2000, for example, an ABCnews.com poll found that two-thirds of Americans supported students' rights to lead school prayers over public address systems at school activities such as sporting events. A year earlier, a Gallup poll had revealed that 70 percent of Americans supported "daily prayer to be spoken in the classroom."[13]

Although school-prayer advocates believe strongly in the benefits of prayer and would like all students to participate, most supporters believe that a compromise solution would be possible. Before the *Engel* decision, it was common practice for schools to allow people whose religion (or atheism) prevented them from participating in the prayer to simply opt out of the activity, by either not participating in the prayers, or by leaving the room during the prayers. In fact, the people who brought the lawsuits in Maryland and Pennsylvania in the *Schempp* case were entitled to sit out the prayers and Bible readings.

Many school-prayer supporters believe that such a rule makes perfect sense, as it accommodates the majority of people who would like prayer in schools, as well as those people who do not wish to participate. Justice Scalia endorsed this model in his dissent in the *Weisman* case:

> To deprive our society of that important unifying mechanism in order to spare the nonbeliever what seems to me the minimal inconvenience of standing, or even sitting in respectful nonparticipation, is as senseless in policy as it is unsupported in law.[14]

Scalia limited his comments to school graduations, recognizing that the graduation is an unusual event and does not occur during instructional time.

Still, many feel that allowing students to opt out of school prayers is a legitimate practice in the classroom as well. For example, Congressman Istook testified in support of his religious freedom amendment:

> Nobody should be forced to participate . . . [b]ut that does not give them the right to show their intolerance by trying to censor their classmates that may want to say [a prayer].[15]

• **If a majority of Americans support school prayer, why have efforts to amend the Constitution to allow it been unsuccessful?**

Many advocates of prayer in public schools disagree with the Supreme Court's rulings that the practice violates the Constitution. Our nation has a long history of prayer, including prayer in schools, and the Supreme Court has not only ignored that position, but ignores the will of the people. Supporters of school prayer believe that it has many benefits and is needed to help stem the nation's public school crisis.

Prayer Does Not Belong in Public Classrooms

Opposition to prayer in public schools comes in many forms. Although supporters often characterize opponents as "atheists" or "Satanists," or blame opposition to school prayer on "the Jews," opposition to school prayer comes from many people who are very committed to their religion, including many Christian religions. Sometimes, parents or students do not have a problem with the content of the prayer, but believe in the principle that the obligation of religious education belongs to families and churches. More frequently, opposition occurs when individuals' beliefs conflict with prayers being recited in public schools.

- **Should public schools be allowed to lead prayers if all parents and students are willing?**

When Lisa Herdahl moved her family from Wisconsin to a small town in Mississippi in 1993, she enrolled five of her children in the only public school available, which accommodated children in kindergarten through the twelfth grade. She was surprised to learn that the public school broadcast prayers over the intercom, allowed prayers to be recited in the classroom, and offered classes about the Bible. When she learned about these practices, she objected—not because she did not believe in Christianity, but because she did not want the school to provide her children's religious education. As she testified to the Judiciary Committee of the U.S. House of Representatives:

> I am a Christian and I am raising my children as Christians. I believe that it is my job as a parent, and not the job of the public schools, to teach my children about religion and prayer. Religion is something that my children learn at home and in church, and I did not and do not want the public schools telling them when and how to pray. Because prayers were being broadcast over the school intercom as classes were beginning in the morning, however, my children could not avoid them. I was particularly concerned because the intercom prayers were in the name of Jesus, and I teach my children to pray directly to God. My ability as a parent to teach my children to pray and our religious freedom was being undermined.[1]

Courts have repeatedly held that the types of activities that Lisa Herdahl described to Congress violate the establishment clause of the Constitution. School-prayer opponents also believe that stories like Lisa Herdahl's demonstrate that, rather than alleviating problems, school prayer creates problems and prevents people from being able to practice their own religion.

Prayer in the classroom violates the establishment clause.

The U.S. Constitution requires a careful balancing act when it comes to religion. The First Amendment reads: "Congress shall make no law respecting an establishment of religion, or prohibiting the free exercise thereof," and is made applicable to the states through the Fourteenth Amendment. Thus, the Constitution appears to put the government in the difficult position of, on the one hand, not furthering religion, and on the other hand, of not impeding it. To school-prayer opponents, however, there is really no conflict: A government can comply with both mandates by erecting a "wall of separation between church and state"—by making no official endorsement of religion and spending no financial or other resources on religious activities.

• Should religion and the state be separated completely?

To opponents of school prayer, public education and prayer are not wholly incompatible. Students can certainly pray on their own, either silently, whenever they wish, or in groups during noninstructional time. According to the American Association of School Administrators, the difference is that voluntary prayers by students are perfectly acceptable, but the prayers must not be organized by the school and must not be forced upon people who do not wish to participate:

> Students across the country are meeting at their school to study the Bible and even to pray at the flagpole. . . . [R]eligion and God can still be a part of raising our children and having them attend public schools.[2]

In a report prepared by People For the American Way Foundation, a Washington, D.C.-based group that opposes organized school prayer, this organization explains:

> The Religious Right axiom that "God has been kicked out of the public schools" is simply not true. Individual students are free to pray and share their faith with others in the same voluntary, non-disruptive manner that they may engage in other speech at school.[3]

Why do school-prayer opponents draw the line at prayers being read by students or teachers in public classrooms? Local, state, and federal government agencies spend a substantial amount of money on public education, making class time a significant government resource. And when class time is dedicated to prayer, a government resource is being used to promote religion. This is more than clear from the decisions of the Supreme Court, which reaffirmed in 2000: "[T]he religious liberty protected by the Constitution is abridged when the State affirmatively sponsors the particular religious practice of prayer."[4] Even if the prayer is composed by students and spoken by students, the prayer violates the Constitution if it takes place in the classroom or at school-sponsored events, such as graduation ceremonies and football games. School-prayer opponents are frustrated by repeated violations of the law by schools all across the country, such as the blatant violations by the school attended by Lisa Herdahl's children.

School-prayer supporters seem unwilling to accept the message that religion does not belong in the classroom. They frequently point to the Pledge of Allegiance, which contains the phrase "one nation, under God," as an example of the important role that religion plays in public life, including the classroom. (Although a federal appeals court in California held in 2002 that reciting the pledge in public schools is unconstitutional, that ruling has been temporarily stayed, and both Congress and the president have sharply criticized the decision.)

> • **Should students recite the Pledge of Allegiance as it stands, including the words "under God"?**

Even if it is accepted that the Pledge of Allegiance is constitutional, opponents of school prayer believe that it is possible to draw the line between the Pledge of Allegiance and school prayer. Although the Pledge of Allegiance recognizes the existence of a divine being, or "God," it is clear that the overriding goal of the Pledge of Allegiance is national unity. Throughout the United States, students recite the same pledge as an activity of patriotism and citizenship. Congress and the courts (with the exception of the three-judge panel in California) have scrutinized the pledge and all agree that it does not have a primarily religious purpose, and there is consensus that it does not favor any particular denomination.

When it comes to individual prayers, however, serious questions are raised whether the prayers are led by students or by teachers. Perhaps the most important question is this: If

FROM THE BENCH

Is the Pledge of Allegiance Unconstitutional?

From *Newdow* v. *United States*, No. 00–16423 (9th Cir. June 26, 2002):

In the context of the Pledge [of Allegiance], the statement that the United States is a nation "under God" is an endorsement of religion. It is a profession of a religious belief, namely, a belief in monotheism. The recitation that ours is a nation "under God" is not a mere acknowledgment that many Americans believe in a deity. Nor is it merely descriptive of the undeniable historical significance of religion in the founding of the Republic. Rather, the phrase "one nation under God" in the context of the Pledge is normative. To recite the Pledge is not to describe the United States; instead, it is to swear allegiance to the values for which the flag stands: unity, indivisibility, liberty, justice, and—since 1954 [when Congress added the phrase "under God" to the Pledge]—monotheism. The text of the official Pledge, codified in federal law, impermissibly takes a position with respect to the purely religious question of the existence and identity of God. A profession that we are a nation "under God" is identical, for Establishment Clause purposes, to a profession that we are a nation "under Jesus," a nation "under Vishnu," a nation "under Zeus," or a nation "under no god," because none of these professions can be neutral with respect to religion....

Although students cannot be forced to participate in recitation of the Pledge, the school district is nonetheless conveying a message of state endorsement of a "nondenominational prayers" are to be acceptable, then who decides whether the prayer used in any given classroom is indeed nondenominational? Does a teacher decide if a prayer favors the Lutheran students in his or her class over the Jewish students? Does a school principal monitor student-led prayers to make sure that the prayers chosen and recited by Islamic students do not offend Baptists?

- **Should students be able to take turns reciting prayers in the classroom, to ensure that all viewpoints are represented?**

religious belief when it requires public school teachers to recite, and lead the recitation of, the current form of the Pledge....

Although the defendants argue that the religious content of "one nation under God" is minimal, to an atheist or a believer in certain non-Judeo-Christian religions or philosophies, it may reasonably appear to be an attempt to enforce a "religious orthodoxy" of monotheism, and is therefore impermissible. The coercive effect of this policy is particularly pronounced in the school setting given the age and impressionability of schoolchildren, and their understanding that they are required to adhere to the norms set by their school, their teacher and their fellow students....

Historically, the primary purpose of the 1954 Act was to advance religion.... The federal defendants "do not dispute that the words 'under God' were intended" "to recognize a Supreme Being, " at a time when the government was publicly inveighing against atheistic communism. Nonetheless, the federal defendants ... claim that the Pledge has the secular purpose of "solemnizing public occasions, expressing confidence in the future, and encouraging the recognition of what is worthy of appreciation in society." ... The flaw in defendants' argument is that it looks at the text of the Pledge "as a whole," and glosses over the 1954 Act.... [T]he legislative history of the 1954 Act reveals that the Act's sole purpose was to advance religion, in order to differentiate the United States from nations under communist rule.... Such a purpose runs counter to the Establishment Clause, which prohibits the government's endorsement or advancement not only of one particular religion at the expense of other religions, but also of religion at the expense of atheism....

The question about whether any given prayer is nonde-nominational is essentially a question of religious doctrine rather than law. And the Supreme Court has made it perfectly clear that the government should not be in the business of deciding questions of religion. As the Court held in *Lee* v. *Weisman*:

> If common ground can be defined which permits once conflicting faiths to express the shared conviction that there is an ethic and a morality which transcend human invention, the sense of community and purpose sought by all decent societies might be advanced. But . . . the First Amendment does not . . . permit the government to undertake that task for itself. . . . These concerns have particular application in the case of school officials, whose effort to monitor prayer will be perceived by the students as inducing a participation they might other-wise reject.[5]

To school-prayer opponents, the answer is simple: Let students pray alone, or outside of class time with completely voluntary and noncoercive religious clubs. Children who wish to pray can then pray in their own way, without the school restricting others' rights. As the trial judge remarked in the Herdahl case, "as long as there are tests in schools there will be prayers there also."[6]

School prayer is not the solution to educational problems.

Opponents of prayer in public schools believe that is unfair to blame problems in public schools on the absence of prayer. They criticize studies such as David Barton's *America: To Pray or Not to Pray*, which documents declining test scores, increased violence, and increased teen pregnancy rates beginning with the abolition of school prayer in the early 1960s. While not denying that significant problems exist, both for public schools and America's youth in general, many opponents of school prayer deny that these problems can be definitively linked to the removal of prayer from public school classrooms. For example, Barton's study points to increases in divorce rates, the number of unmarried couples living together, and alcohol consumption; it is difficult to make the connection between the elimination of school prayer and problems that affect mostly adults. People who had already reached adulthood in 1963 had attended schools in which the Supreme Court had not yet barred school prayer.

Rob Boston of Americans United for Separation of Church and State has criticized Barton's writings as "pseudo-scientific" and writes, "In reality, the drop in SAT scores can be attributed to the fact that these days a wider variety of students from a broader range of socioeconomic backgrounds take the test, not just well-off kids from the suburbs as was common in the 1950s."[7] Many other factors have changed since 1962, and not all of the changes can be attributed to the lack of prayer in schools, school prayer opponents believe. School-prayer opponents believe that religious upbringing is the responsibility of the family, not the public schools. Some of the very factors that are mentioned in Barton's study—divorce rates and number of single-parent households—point to less time spent together as a family, which presumably means less time for prayer. Other factors that explain the increase in teen sexuality (e.g., pregnancies and sexually transmitted diseases) include the widespread availability of the birth control pill in the early 1960s and the nationwide legalization of abortion in 1972.

- **What other events of the 1960s may have led to some of the effects described in Barton's report?**

Thursday, June 27, 2002: Kindergarten students recite the Pledge of Allegiance at Florence Markofer Elementary School in Elk Grove, California. On June 26, the U.S. Court of Appeals for the Ninth Circuit, responding to a lawsuit filed by a parent of one of the school's students, ruled the Pledge of Allegiance unconstitutional because it contained the words "under God." This decision has caused a firestorm of criticism and generally has not been implemented in schools. Opponents stress that the purpose of the words is to promote national unity, rather than to imply the U.S. government's affiliation with any religious system. Both President George W. Bush and the U.S. Congress have joined in criticizing the judgment.

School prayer harms individual students and parents.

For school-prayer opponents, the answer to the argument that many students, parents, and educators support school prayer is simple: The protection of minority religious views is exactly why the Constitution prohibits the government from endorsing any particular view of religion. As federal trial Judge Neal Biggers explained in *Herdahl* v. *Pontotoc County School District* (1996):

> The District's witnesses testified that the school prayers should continue because a majority of the students and parents are in favor of the practice and Mrs. Herdahl is the only person who opposes the practice; however, the Bill of Rights was created to protect the minority from tyranny by the majority. Indeed, without the benefit of such a document, women in this country have been burned because the majority of their townspeople believed their religious practices were contrary to the tenets of funda-mentalist Christianity. To say that the majority should prevail simply because of its numbers is to forget the purpose of the Bill of Rights.[8]

School-prayer supporters frequently argue that allowing students to opt out of classroom prayer saves them from any harm that may occur from a prayer that offends either their religious beliefs or their lack of religious beliefs. However, the solution of allowing students to "opt out" is unacceptable to school-prayer opponents. The main problem with this approach, they say, is that students are extremely impressionable, and, therefore, may be coerced by classmates to join in prayers that offend their own—or their parents'—religious belief system.

> • **Does the First Amendment apply to communities in which there are no minority viewpoints to protect?**

The coercive effect is made even greater by the ridicule, scorn, or even threats, that nonparticipating students often must face. The experience of Lisa Herdahl's family illustrates why "opting out" is not a solution:

> Because I requested that my children not participate in the religious instruction at the school, my children have been

ridiculed and harassed by teachers and classmates, and falsely called "devil worshipers" and "atheists." For example, as my son David was leaving his elementary classroom before one Bible class, one of his classmates also asked to leave the classroom. His teacher said words to the effect that: "David doesn't believe in God. People who believe in God go to Bible class—those who don't, don't go to Bible class." David was later harassed by other children who falsely accused him of not believing in God.

On another occasion last year, when my son Jason was seven years old and in the second grade, his teacher placed headphones on his head so that he would not hear the prayers coming over the intercom. After the teacher put the headphones on Jason's head, his classmates responded by calling him "football head" and "baseball head." Jason, who is now eight, has continued to be called names by his classmates and to be thumped on the head and grabbed by the ears. It is no wonder that he sometimes does not want to go to school in the morning. . . .

[I]n order to protect my children, I had no choice but to file a lawsuit in federal court to stop the school's unconstitutional practices. As a result, the harassment of my family got even worse. Signs appeared all over town in support of the school's practices. I personally have received a death threat in the mail and my family has received bomb threats.[9]

• **How can a school control its students' intolerance of others' religious beliefs?**

Lisa Herdahl, who professes the Christian faith, was the sole objector to the fundamentalist Christian viewpoints being preached in a small Mississippi town. However, in many school districts across the nation, religious viewpoints are much more diverse. School-prayer opponents frequently point to our nation's increasing diversity as a reason not to put much stock in the argument that prayer is part of American heritage. As Justice William Brennan noted in *Schempp*:

> [O]ur religious composition makes us a vastly more diverse people than were our forefathers. They knew differences chiefly among Protestant sects. Today the Nation is far more heterogeneous religiously, including as it does substantial minorities not only of Catholics and Jews but as well of those who worship according to no version of the Bible and those who worship no God at all. . . . In the face of such profound changes, practices which may have been objectionable to no one in the time of Jefferson and Madison may today be highly offensive to many persons, the deeply devout and the nonbelievers alike.[10]

The diversity of the United States' population serves as perhaps the most powerful argument against an amendment to the Constitution allowing school prayer. Religious tolerance is an important factor in the development of our diverse society, which distinguishes the United States from countries in which members of minority religious groups are discriminated against or even killed. Opponents of school prayer fear that any efforts, intended or unintended, to suppress religious diversity will lead to tragic results.

***

Despite the Supreme Court's clear message that organized prayer does not belong in classrooms or at events such as graduations and football games, people in schools across the nation continue to be subjected to prayers that do not support their own religious beliefs. Not only does school prayer violate the establishment clause of the Constitution, but it also can do great harm to individual students.

Religious Clubs in Public Schools Should Be Treated More Fairly

Although the Supreme Court's rulings have essentially eliminated prayer from public school classrooms, religion still has a major place in public schools in the form of religious clubs devoted to Bible study, fellowship, and other activities. The significant differences are that participation in these clubs is voluntary, that the school does not lead them, and that they take place outside of ordinary class time. Yet, religious clubs often encounter resistance from administrators, and supporters believe that the clubs should be treated more fairly.

School systems frequently violate students' equal access rights.

Religious clubs enjoy protections from two important legal sources. The first is the First Amendment to the Constitution. Interestingly, it is not the amendment's religion clauses that provide protection for religious clubs in public schools, but the free speech clause of the First Amendment. A long line of Supreme Court decisions has held that schools may not discriminate against what a club has to say simply because it has a religious viewpoint. In *Widmar* v. *Vincent,* the Court held that the University of Missouri at Kansas City, which had allowed various student groups to meet on campus, had created a "open forum" and could not discriminate against groups that had a religious basis:

> Through its policy of accommodating . . . meetings, the University has created a forum generally open for use by student groups. Having done so, the University has assumed an obligation to justify its discriminations and exclusions under applicable constitutional norms. . . . The Constitution forbids a State to enforce certain exclusions from a forum generally open to the public, even if it was not required to create the forum in the first place. . . .
>
> Here [the University] has discriminated against student groups and speakers based on their desire to use a generally open forum to engage in religious worship and discussion. These are forms of speech and association protected by the First Amendment.[1]

> • **Should schools be able to censor their students? What if a student-run club advocated drug use?**

Although the *Widmar* case dealt specifically with a university setting, Congress acted to ensure that high schools also would not discriminate against religious clubs. In 1984, Congress passed the Equal Access Act,[2] which requires that any high school receiving federal funding must allow religious groups to meet (outside of classroom time) "whenever such school grants an offering to or opportunity for one or more noncurriculum-related student groups to meet on school premises during non-instructional time."[3] In *Westside Community Board of Education*

v. *Mergens*,[4] the Supreme Court interpreted the act to mean that if a school allows a chess club to form, then it must also allow a Bible club to form. Also, in *Good News Club* v. *Milford Central School*,[5] the Court held that a school could not exclude an after-school program designed for elementary schoolchildren.

Although the Equal Access Act and the Supreme Court's

THE LETTER OF THE LAW

Federal Law Prohibits Discrimination Against Religious Clubs in High Schools

From The Equal Access Act, 20 U.S.C. §§4071–4074:

§4071.—Denial of equal access prohibited

(a) Restriction of limited open forum on basis of religious, political, philosophical, or other speech content prohibited

It shall be unlawful for any public secondary school which receives Federal financial assistance and which has a limited open forum to deny equal access or a fair opportunity to, or discriminate against, any students who wish to conduct a meeting within that limited open forum on the basis of the religious, political, philosophical, or other content of the speech at such meetings.

(b) "Limited open forum" defined

A public secondary school has a limited open forum whenever such school grants an offering to or opportunity for one or more non-curriculum related student groups to meet on school premises during noninstructional time.

(c) Fair opportunity criteria

Schools shall be deemed to offer a fair opportunity to students who wish to conduct a meeting within its limited open forum if such school uniformly provides that—

(1) the meeting is voluntary and student-initiated;

(2) there is no sponsorship of the meeting by the school, the government, or its agents or employees;

(3) employees or agents of the school or government are present at religious meetings only in a nonparticipatory capacity;

(4) the meeting does not materially and substantially interfere with the orderly conduct of educational activities within the school; and

decisions provide a fairly simple rule protecting the rights of students to form religious clubs, schools throughout the nation frequently deny students the right to form Bible clubs and other religious clubs.[6] For example, in March of 2001, an appeals court in California ruled that Mission Viejo High School had wrongfully excluded a chapter of the Fellowship of Christian Athletes. Later

(5) nonschool persons may not direct, conduct, control, or regularly attend activities of student groups.

(d) Construction of subchapter with respect to certain rights

Nothing in this subchapter shall be construed to authorize the United States or any State or political subdivision thereof—

(1) to influence the form or content of any prayer or other religious activity;

(2) to require any person to participate in prayer or other religious activity;

(3) to expend public funds beyond the incidental cost of providing the space for student-initiated meetings;

(4) to compel any school agent or employee to attend a school meeting if the content of the speech at the meeting is contrary to the beliefs of the agent or employee;

(5) to sanction meetings that are otherwise unlawful;

(6) to limit the rights of groups of students which are not of a specified numerical size; or

(7) to abridge the constitutional rights of any person.

(e) Federal financial assistance to schools unaffected

Notwithstanding the availability of any other remedy under the Constitution or the laws of the United States, nothing in this subchapter shall be construed to authorize the United States to deny or withhold Federal financial assistance to any school.

(f) Authority of schools with respect to order, discipline, well-being, and attendance concerns

Nothing in this subchapter shall be construed to limit the authority of the school, its agents or employees, to maintain order and discipline on school premises, to protect the well-being of students and faculty, and to assure that attendance of students at meetings is voluntary.

that year, facing legal pressure, another California school district changed its policy, allowing religious clubs to distribute promotional materials at school; the controversy arose when school officials prevented members of the All About Him club from hanging posters containing the word "God." An attorney for the group remarked, "The issue was whether the literature was disruptive to the students' learning environment, which it clearly was not."[7]

At the same time and in a similar case, a Louisiana school system denied a student the right to start a Bible club and a Fellowship of Christian Athletes chapter. The local school board wrote to Dominique Begnaud that to maintain the separation of church and state, she should hold these meetings at her home or at a church. Acting upon this clear violation of the Equal Access Act, Orlando-based Liberty Counsel took up Begnaud's legal case, and the school district relented. Said Mathew D. Staver of Liberty Counsel:

> It is hard to understand why schools cannot get the message of equal access. The Equal Access law has been in existence since 1984 and its message is crystal clear. Equal access means equal treatment. If school administrators can't understand the simple message of equal access, you wonder how they can teach children anything. When a school prohibits a club solely because of its religious content, the school violates the First Amendment provision that it pretends to uphold.[8]

Truly equal access includes access to funding and activities during the school day.

Under the Equal Access Act, there are certain restrictions placed upon students' rights to form religious clubs. For example, the act does not require school systems to provide any funding in excess of the incidental cost of providing meeting space. Additionally, the act allows clubs to meet during "time set aside by the school before actual classroom instruction begins or after actual classroom instruction ends."[9] However, many people have questioned whether these limitations imposed by the

Equal Access Act are fair—how can access be "equal" if these limits are not also imposed on secular clubs? Students have begun to use the court system to ensure that equal access is truly equal. For example, in the *Good News Club* case, the Supreme Court held that even though the Equal Access Act does not apply to elementary schools, that the First Amendment's free speech protections prevented a school from allowing some outside speakers, but not a religious group.

> • **Should a school spend money on clubs in which not all students can participate? What if a school had a sports team that excluded people of a certain religion?**

While some lower courts have issued rulings that have helped make religious groups' access to schools "more equal," neither Congress nor the Supreme Court has provided truly equal access to religious clubs, which many believe is tantamount to religious discrimination. For example, in most states, because the Equal Access Act applies to times before or after actual classroom instruction, schools are able to allow secular clubs to meet during lunchtime, but may not allow religious clubs to do so as well. This clearly amounts to treating religious and secular clubs differently. The federal Court of Appeals for the Ninth Circuit—in a decision affecting several Western states— held that lunchtime *was* "before or after actual instructional time," and therefore the Equal Access Act applies,[10] and many commentators have praised this decision in hopes that it will be adopted nationwide. Still, some would like to see the decision taken a step further: If student groups such as the school newspaper and yearbook meet during class time, then perhaps religious clubs should have the same opportunity, even though the Equal Access Act does not impose such a requirement.

Another Ninth Circuit decision that has inspired supporters of religious clubs is *Prince* v. *Jacoby*.[11] In that case, the Court ruled that a school that allows secular clubs to benefit from student activity fees, audiovisual equipment, school vehicles, and other benefits of financial value cannot deny these same benefits to religious clubs. Again, many observers applauded the decision for addressing what they perceived to be the unfairness of denying school funding—as endorsed by the Equal Access Act—to religious clubs.

Supporters of religious clubs hope that the principles of the Ninth Circuit's decisions will be adopted throughout the United States, but there are still additional ways in which the Equal Access Act provides access that is not truly equal. For example, under the act, teachers are allowed to be "present at religious meetings only in a nonparticipatory capacity." The same limitation certainly does not apply to sports teams or drama clubs, for example. Additionally, under the act, "nonschool persons may not direct, conduct, control, or regularly attend activities of student groups," although an outside karate master or art teacher might be allowed to train students. To many, the limitations imposed by the Equal Access Act are tantamount to discrimination

FROM THE BENCH

Religious Clubs in Elementary Schools

**From *Good News Club* v. *Milford Central School*,
No. 99–2036 (June 11, 2001):**

We are guided in our analysis by two of our prior opinions, *Lamb's Chapel* and *Rosenberger*. In *Lamb's Chapel*, we held that a school district violated the Free Speech Clause of the First Amendment when it excluded a private group from presenting films at the school based solely on the films' discussions of family values from a religious perspective. Likewise, in *Rosenberger*, we held that a university's refusal to fund a student publication because the publication addressed issues from a religious perspective violated the Free Speech Clause. Concluding that Milford's exclusion of the Good News Club based on its religious nature is indistinguishable from the exclusions in these cases, we hold that the exclusion constitutes viewpoint discrimination....

Milford has opened its limited public forum to activities that serve a variety of purposes, including events "pertaining to the welfare of the community."... Milford interprets its policy to permit discussions of subjects such as child rearing, and of "the development of character and morals from a religious perspective."...

against a religious viewpoint. For example, Peter J. Ferrara has advocated for a "no-discrimination doctrine," under which "[r]eligious speakers would be allowed on campus to the same extent as other speakers."[12]

Allowing clubs to meet is not endorsing religion.

A frequent reason cited by schools for excluding or limiting the activities of Bible clubs and other religious clubs is that allowing them to operate violates the principle of separation of church and state. For example, this was the reason given by the Louisiana school for denying Dominique Begnaud the opportunity to start religious clubs at her school, and it has also been the defense of school systems involved in important litigation such as *Mergens* and *Good News Club*. However, it is clear from legal precedent that separation of church and state does not require the exclusion of religious clubs.

For example, this policy would allow someone to use Aesop's Fables to teach children moral values.... Additionally, a group could sponsor a debate on whether there should be a constitutional amendment to permit prayer in public schools ... and the Boy Scouts could meet "to influence a boy's character, development and spiritual growth."... In short, any group that "promote[s] the moral and character development of children" is eligible to use the school building....

Just as there is no question that teaching morals and character development to children is a permissible purpose under Milford's policy, it is clear that the Club teaches morals and character development to children. For example, no one disputes that the Club instructs children to overcome feelings of jealousy, to treat others well regardless of how they treat the children, and to be obedient, even if it does so in a nonsecular way. Nonetheless, because Milford found the Club's activities to be religious in nature—"the equivalent of religious instruction itself," ... it excluded the Club from use of its facilities....

When Milford denied the Good News Club access to the school's limited public forum on the ground that the Club was religious in nature, it discriminated against the Club because of its religious viewpoint in violation of the Free Speech Clause of the First Amendment.

• Do schools favor some clubs over others?

Frequently, the argument is stated in terms of a school's desire to avoid "endorsing" religion in general or supporting and endorsing any specific religion. Still, the idea that allowing religious clubs to meet under the Equal Access Act amounts to an endorsement of religion was soundly rejected by the Supreme Court in *Mergens*:

> [P]etitioners maintain that because the school's recognized student activities are an integral part of its educational mission, official recognition of respondents' proposed club would effectively incorporate religious activities into the school's official program, endorse participation in the religious club, and provide the club with an official platform to proselytize other students.
>
> We disagree. . . . Indeed, the message is one of neutrality rather than endorsement; if a State refused to let religious groups use facilities open to others, then it would demonstrate not neutrality but hostility toward religion.[13]

Despite the clarity of the Supreme Court's pronouncement, the same "endorsement" defense was raised a decade later by the school system in *Good News Club*, and was again rejected:

> There is no evidence that young children are permitted to loiter outside classrooms after the schoolday has ended. Surely even young children are aware of events for which their parents must sign permission forms. The meetings were held in a combined high school resource room and middle school special education room, not in an elementary school classroom. The instructors are not schoolteachers. And the children in the group are not all the same age as in the normal classroom setting; their ages range from 6 to 12. . . . In sum, these circumstances simply do not support the theory that small children would perceive endorsement here.[14]

Although many administrators might fear that religious clubs will create an appearance that the school is endorsing religion, the answer is not to exclude the clubs. Rather, suggests the Anti-Defamation League:

> School officials must protect against such impressions, and may do so by issuing disclaimers clearly stating that the school is not sponsoring, endorsing or promoting any non-curriculum-related student groups.[15]

In its brief to the Supreme Court in *Good News Club*, a group of states' attorneys general had the following suggestion:

> If Respondent was worried that parents or other adults might misunderstand the school's constitutionally mandated neutrality toward religion, it could explain its position to them. If the school was concerned that younger children still might be confused, it could use the opportunity as a first civics lesson and explain to them, in age-appropriate terms, its neutral position. Even young children can understand the concept of neutrality from the role of referees and umpires in sports and playground games, and Respondent could describe its role in similar terms.[16]

- **What happens when a popular teacher—or a popular student—supports a particular club?**

Although the Equal Access Act was a step in the right direction, many supporters of religious clubs believe that the clubs still do not have truly equal access. They would like to see religious clubs have access to funding and class time, and do not think that such support violates the Constitution.

Religious Clubs in Public Schools Have Unfair Advantages

Despite the Equal Access Act and the Supreme Court's decisions in the *Mergens* and *Good News Club* cases, many people have expressed concerns with both the way that the Equal Access Act is written and the way that it is applied in public schools. Both atheists and members of minority religious groups are concerned that the presence of religious clubs in public schools can lead to religious oppression.

- Is atheism a religious belief? If not, then are the opinions of atheists as important as religious beliefs? Is it fair to require students to suppress their religious beliefs while at public school?

Religious clubs belong in houses of worship, not in public schools.

Although many mainstream religious organizations support

Students at a high school in Garden City, Kansas, gather to pray on a September morning in 2000. The gathering was part of a student-run international campaign called "See You at the Pole," which calls on students to pray at their school's flagpole on a given date each year. Meetings such as this generally are considered acts of free speech on public grounds.

the Equal Access Act and the presence of religious clubs in public schools, many other people believe that the public schools are simply not appropriate places for religious activity.

Ellen Johnson, president of the New Jersey–based American Atheists organization, writes:

> [E]ven though there are 350,000 churches, mosques, temples, chapels, and other "houses of worship" in the United States, giving religious believers ample opportunity to practice their faiths, our public schools remained battlegrounds over the separation of church and state.[1]

A major problem with allowing religious groups to form in public schools, Johnson believes, is that the various provisions of the Equal Access Act and related federal guidelines are "exploited for loopholes" by people trying to advance a particular religious agenda. In other words, the complicated set of guidelines set up by the Equal Access Act, court decisions, and federal regulations makes it difficult or impossible to monitor which activities fall within the guidelines and which do not. Johnson suggests that a complete prohibition on religious activities in school would eliminate many problems:

> There would be no need for "guidelines" and "reports," and there would be no "problem" if those who practice religion confined their activities to churches, temples, mosques, and other houses of worship, or to the privacy of their own homes and voluntary gatherings. . . . Religious practices in the public schools have necessitated constant litigation and protest.[2]

An example of a loophole that is frequently exploited by people trying to advance a religious agenda is the fact that the requirement in the Equal Access Act that groups be "student-initiated"[3] is not carefully defined. The result, writes Johnson, is that "many religious activities which are defended as 'student-led' or 'student-initiated' are, in fact, the results of organized efforts by adult, off-campus groups." [4] She gives the example of widespread group prayers in response to the Supreme Court's 2000 decision in *Santa Fe Independent School District* v. *Doe* (which banned organized prayer at high school football games) by claiming that the group prayers were the result of "bullying" by "off-campus ministers, religious groups, or churches."

The literature and publicity campaigns of youth ministry organizations reaffirm that the concerns of the American Atheists are quite real. Many religious organizations actively use adults to bring religion into public schools. For example, as reported in the *Baptist Standard*,[5] evangelist Fred Lynch urged Texans to become active in "a national movement to establish student-initiated prayer and evangelism ministries on all 56,000 secondary school campuses in the United States." Although referring to "student-initiated, student-led campus clubs," Lynch stressed the need to link "maturing Christian teenagers to mature Christian adults" and that youth ministers should "train adult volunteers as off-campus coaches who mentor a small group of campus missionaries."

• **What problems might arise from allowing adults to direct the activities of student clubs?**

Although the groups envisioned by Lynch might be started by a student asking his or her school for permission to start a club, many people are disturbed by the fact that churches or adult lay ministers might be the driving force behind starting the club, might direct the group's basic tenets, and might continue to shape the group's operations, activities, and beliefs. To some people, this practice seems to run afoul of the Equal Access Act's requirement that "nonschool persons may not direct, conduct, control, or regularly attend activities of student groups." [6] Yet, by using adults who meet with student leaders outside of school, the

ministries are able to comply with the "letter of the law"—
or are at least able to escape detection. This is the type of
loophole that American Atheists has criticized.

Insight into just how much control adults can have
over supposedly "student-initiated, student-led groups" is
provided by the literature of the Orlando, Florida–based
Coaching Center. Through a network of adult and youth
ministers, the Coaching Center provides guidance to
students in forming religious clubs in schools. On the
organization's website, a discussion of "involving adults in
ministry" cautions:

> If you are a student, do yourself a favor and get an adult
> to take on this responsibility! In most cases they will
> enjoy it and have more success. Even if you are able to
> delegate this aspect of your ministry you need to read
> this and understand how valuable adults are to reaching
> your school.[7]

Another national group, Fun with Faith Clubs, Inc.,
identifies and trains parents to start religious clubs in
elementary schools and educate children about the group's
interpretation of scripture:

> [A] Christian parent volunteers his or her time to build
> the spiritual foundation of their child and classmates. A
> Christian parent is identified . . . as one who . . . [h]as made
> a public confession that Jesus Christ is their personal
> Lord and Savior and . . . [b]elieves the Bible is the true,
> complete Word of God, inspired by the Holy Spirit, and
> without error.[8]

• **Are there ways for parents to "protect" their children from adopting different religious beliefs?**

The greatest concern of many people who oppose religious clubs in schools is that children—especially elementary school students, but, also high school students—are very impressionable. Opponents of such clubs believe that parents, or religious leaders of the parents' choosing, should be responsible for children's religious education. Many have concerns that other adults—whether by appearing in school or by acting through a student intermediary—should have the opportunity to present religious beliefs that conflict with those taught by children's own parents.

In dissenting from a federal court decision that allowed a religious club to meet at a public school during lunchtime, federal Judge Donald P. Lay wrote:

> [P]arents wield little effective control over their children during the regular school day. . . . Unlike before or after school, most parents are unable to keep their children away from activities during the lunch period. . . . Thus, their children may be confronted by or participate in religious expression in the public schools that parents find offensive or harmful but from which they are unable to shield their children. . . . Student-initiated religious meetings during the school day, potentially led by student evangelists (or worse), threaten to violate the trust that parents place in schools not to usurp the family's role in inculcating religious values protected by the Constitution.[9]

Religious clubs interfere with instruction and divert resources from other students.

Many parents, students, and others are concerned that despite the restrictions placed upon religious clubs by the Equal Access Act—such as provisions limiting club activities to non-instructional time and prohibiting the expenditure of school funds—that religious clubs interfere with the education of nonparticipating students. The decision in *Ceniceros* v. *Board of Trustees of San Diego Unified School District,* from which Judge Lay dissented, is an example of how the Equal Access Act has been slowly expanded by case law, allowing religious groups even greater latitude to operate in public schools. Although the Equal Access Act limits club activities to "noninstructional time," defined as "time set aside by the school before actual classroom instruction begins or after actual classroom instruction ends," [10] the *Ceniceros* court interpreted this to mean lunchtime.

Decisions allowing religious activities during the school day—rather than before classes start or after the last bell rings—indicate a dangerous precedent to people who support a strong separation of church and state. Although activities at lunchtime might not take away from "instructional time" in the classroom, they certainly can have a disruptive effect on the education of students, particularly those who do not care to hear the messages. As Judge Lay noted in his dissent, "Students who are exposed to religious meetings in a close and closed environment may find it hard to refuse because they cannot just walk away from the premises." [11]

• **Does the lunch hour count as "before or after" instructional time?**

The *Ceniceros* decision sets up a legal slippery slope in which more and more activities could be condoned because they do not interfere with actual class instruction. If a religious group is allowed to meet during lunchtime, then would members of the group be allowed to hand out religious tracts or preach to fellow students who are waiting in line to buy their lunches? Would members be allowed to stand at classroom doorways handing literature to students entering or leaving the classroom? Many parts of the school day are subject to claims of being "noninstructional time," such as recess for elementary school students, or the time in which older students change and shower before and after physical education classes. Although these times are not set aside for instruction per se, a student who is subjected to unwanted proselytizing during the school day might find it more difficult to concentrate on his or her classes.

Although some of the hypothetical situations mentioned above might sound unrealistic, groups are already using such tactics to spread their religious message beyond the confines of a closed meeting of interested students. For example, Teens 4 Jesus Youth Ministries advises its members:

> Instead of holing up in your sponsor's classroom take your group outside. Meet in the cafeteria, in a large grassy area like a quad, in the library, at the front of the school, etc. Let others know where you will be meeting by including it in the school announcements or by passing out or hanging fliers. . . . Ask your principal if perhaps you can set up a prayer box in the cafeteria or library. Invite other students to share prayer requests in the box.[12]

The methods of publicizing club activities such as those advocated by Teens 4 Jesus have raised concerns. It is often difficult for schools to draw the line between publicizing club activities, which is permissible under the Equal Access Act, and evangelizing, which is not. After Lisa Herdahl brought a lawsuit against her children's Mississippi school for broadcasting prayers over the school intercom, the officially sanctioned prayers were replaced by prayers led by a student club. The school defended its actions by claiming that it was merely allowing the club to publicize its activities:

> Prior to this court's preliminary injunction, the District contended that its stated policy and practice on the issue of school-wide prayer over the intercom was that the Center would permit student clubs or organizations brief

access to the public address system, following the morning announcements by the administration, for the purpose of making any student announcement or any other free speech comments the students desire. The Aletheia Club, formerly the Christ In Us Club, one of the recognized student clubs at the school, had frequently utilized this period of time to present a short devotional, or inspirational message, which often included a short Bible reading, frequently followed by a short prayer. The entire devotional and prayer generally lasted no longer than a minute or two. During this period, teachers directed students who were standing to be seated and directed students who were talking to be quiet, if necessary, and at least some teachers in their classrooms bowed their heads for the prayers and devotionals.[13]

Herdahl objected to her children's being exposed to these prayers on the morning announcements because they did not reflect her own Christian religious beliefs. Although she prevailed in her lawsuit and succeeded in having such practices banned in that particular Mississippi school, the fact that the litigation occurred is evidence that the freedoms provided by the Equal Access Act and *Good News Club* decision can be misused to expose students to religious messages that are contrary to those of some students and their parents.

> • **Should religious clubs be allowed to pray over public address systems? Should math clubs be allowed to discuss geometry?**

In the same way that the Equal Access Act's limitation of religious activities to "noninstructional time" presents opportunities for abuse, there is similar danger for abuse of the act's statement that schools are not required "to expend public funds beyond the incidental cost of providing the space for student-initiated meetings."[14] In fact, a federal

Lisa Herdahl was shocked to find that the public schools in her town were permitting prayer and even offering classes about the Bible; as a Christian, she wanted the responsibility for her children's religious education to stay with her family. When she objected, she and her children faced harassment, and finally she filed suit. In this image, Jerry Horton, superintendent of schools for Pontohoc County, Mississippi, passes Herdahl supporters (and hymn-singing students) outside the Mississippi federal courthouse in which the case was tried. On Monday, March 4, 1996, the federal judge who heard the case ordered an end to the school's 50-year tradition of organized prayer and Bible study.

appeals court in San Francisco ruled in *Prince* v. *Jacoby*[15] that a school that allowed the expenditure of student activity fees (which were collected through fundraising and individual contributions) for nonreligious clubs could not deny expenditure of these funds for religious clubs. Perhaps more disturbing to advocates of separation of church and state was the Court's ruling that although the Equal Access Act does not require the expenditure of public funds for religious clubs, the First Amendment's free speech protections do:

> [T]he World Changers seek nothing more than to be treated neutrally and given access to speak about the same topics as other groups. . . . That the provision of school supplies and school vehicles in this case involves public, rather than [school activity], funds does not change our consideration. . . . [W]e hold that the First Amendment requires that the school district grant the World Changers equal access to the school yearbook, audio/visual equipment, school supplies, and school vehicles.

The standard established by the Court is ripe for abuse because it is unclear how much support school districts must provide to religious groups. If the school provides a bus for the football team to play in the state championship 200 miles away, must it also provide a bus for a Bible club to attend a religious revival meeting 200 miles away? Providing transportation can be very expensive, and school districts have limited financial resources. Depending on how the *Prince* decision is interpreted, there is a good possibility that schools will expend significant resources on religious activities, a requirement not foreseen by Congress and seemingly in conflict with the Supreme Court's school-prayer jurisprudence.

Support of religious clubs can convey an endorsement of religion.

Although supporters of religious clubs often claim—as the World Changers did in the *Prince* case—that all they want is "equal access," many people are concerned that in many cases, "equal access" is impossible. In areas in which most people share a single religion, formation of public school clubs embracing that religion can be isolating for students who do not share that religion, and might even convey the idea that the school itself is endorsing a particular religious viewpoint. The danger of creating a sense of endorsement is especially great if teachers appear to support the activities; students have difficulty differentiating between what teachers do in their professional capacity and what they do based on their personal beliefs. Some people believe that court decisions holding that support of school clubs do not amount to endorsement are naïve because in some places, communities are dominated by a particular religious denomination.

> • **Does it make sense for a court to grant to student organizations greater protections than allowed by the Equal Access Act? How specific *is* the Equal Access Act?**

Although the United States is very diverse in religious affiliation, many areas are not quite as diverse. For example, the American Religion Data Archive, operated by Pennsylvania State University, reports that approximately 89 percent of people living in Utah are affiliated with the Church of Jesus Christ of Latter-day Saints (often referred to as the Mormon church.)[16] And in the Mississippi town where Lisa Herdahl moved with her children, most people shared views of Christianity that were different from her own. When the Aletheia Club took over from the school the duties of leading morning prayers, it was clear that the school was strongly supporting the club's activities:

[E]xcluding the Aletheia Club, the intercom was used only for announcements of club activities, including announcements to encourage students to participate in activities, and not for the actual conduct of substantive club activities themselves. For example, the yearbook staff has made announcements over the intercom that it will

meet at designated times and places, but it has not conducted the substance of its meeting over the intercom.
The Aletheia Club, however, has not only announced the
times and places of its meetings over the intercom, it also
has said the prayers and read the devotionals that it gives
in its meetings.[17]

The Anti-Defamation League has expressed concern for
people who, like Lisa Herdahl's children, attend schools in which
religious clubs are elevated to the point in which participation
seems to be a requirement of attending school:

> Schools must also recognize and guard against the threat of
> coercive peer pressure, which may be substantial. Student

FROM THE BENCH

Is Religion out of Place in Public Elementary Schools?

From *Good News Club* v. *Milford Central School*,
No. 99–2036 (June 11, 2001) (Stevens, J., dissenting):

The Milford Central School has invited the public to use its facilities for educational and recreational purposes, but not for "religious purposes." Speech for
"religious purposes" may reasonably be understood to encompass three different
categories. First, there is religious speech that is simply speech about a particular
topic from a religious point of view. . . . Second, there is religious speech that
amounts to worship, or its equivalent. . . . Third, there is an intermediate category
that is aimed principally at proselytizing or inculcating belief in a particular
religious faith. . . .

   [W]hile a public entity may not censor speech about an authorized topic based
on the point of view expressed by the speaker, it has broad discretion to "preserve
the property under its control for the use to which it is lawfully dedicated." . . .
"A school's extracurricular activities constitute a part of the school's teaching
mission, and the school accordingly must make 'decisions concerning the content
of those activities.'" . . .

club members may be able to coerce students into joining sectarian groups, and adhering to the club's beliefs, particularly if the student body is composed largely of the same religious faith as that practiced by club members. Such clubs might create "insider" and "outsider" student groups, and, as a result, students may be ridiculed, harassed or ostracized.[18]

In criticizing the majority's decision in the *Ceniceros* case, Judge Lay echoed the Anti-Defamation League's concerns:

State involvement in recognizing student religious groups during the school day may create greater divisiveness and

Distinguishing speech from a religious viewpoint, on the one hand, from religious proselytizing, on the other, is comparable to distinguishing meetings to discuss political issues from meetings whose principal purpose is to recruit new members to join a political organization. If a school decides to authorize after school discussions of current events in its classrooms, it may not exclude people from expressing their views simply because it dislikes their particular political opinions. But must it therefore allow organized political groups—for example, the Democratic Party, the Libertarian Party, or the Ku Klux Klan—to hold meetings, the principal purpose of which is not to discuss the current-events topic from their own unique point of view but rather to recruit others to join their respective groups? I think not. Such recruiting meetings may introduce divisiveness and tend to separate young children into cliques that undermine the school's educational mission....

School officials may reasonably believe that evangelical meetings designed to convert children to a particular religious faith pose the same risk. And, just as a school may allow meetings to discuss current events from a political perspective without also allowing organized political recruitment, so too can a school allow discussion of topics such as moral development from a religious (or nonreligious) perspective without thereby opening its forum to religious proselytizing or worship....

intolerance toward others who must sit back and idly watch. In many of our public schools the children are predominantly of the Christian faith. Tolerance to other religious or nonreligious beliefs, the essence of the Free Exercise Clause, may fall to the wayside if schools are required to recognize a majoritarian student religious group that advertises and promotes meetings over the lunch break. The resulting ostracism of the minority students who cannot take part is humiliating and offends recognized constitutional principles.[19]

Schools must ensure that respected teachers, coaches, principles, and others do not create an appearance that the school endorses a particular religion. "[I]t is likely that students will misperceive the school's 'custodial' oversight of religious activities that the [Equal Access] Act permits . . . for approval, participation, or even endorsement," wrote Judge Lay. Certainly, youth ministries have targeted teachers and coaches as people who can share a religious message. For example, the Coaching Center advises:

> Christian teachers, coaches and administrators can be a tremendous resource in trying to reach a campus with the gospel, especially if they are well liked and respected among the students and faculty. . . . [Even] with the "perceived" legal limitations . . . [t]hey can be "salt and light" in the classroom. They are within their legal rights by having and defending a biblical worldview.[20]

> • **What limits, if any, should there be on teachers' expressions of their own religious beliefs?**

The ever-blurring line between what is a student-initiated club and what is a school-sponsored religious activity that violates the establishment clause of the First Amendment has led many to call for an end to "voluntary" religious activity. In the words of American Atheists President Ellen Johnson:

> Too much was (and is) being done to magnify the issue of religion in our schools and to find some way of injecting religious themes, activities, organizations, and content into what should, ideally, be secular institutions which have the primary goal of educating students and preparing them for societal integration and the workforce.[21]

Despite the Equal Access Act and Supreme Court decisions, many people believe that religious clubs do not belong in public schools. Opponents are especially concerned that religious clubs take up limited financial resources and educational time. In some areas in which a particular religious viewpoint dominates, the school's support of the clubs effectively endorses the majority religious viewpoint.

Schools Should Teach Theories Other Than Evolution

The public controversy surrounding the theory of evolution developed by Charles Darwin and others is almost as old as the theory itself. Evolution, which theorizes that humans developed from "lower" organisms is in direct conflict with the biblical account of creation, in which God created Adam and Eve. Fundamentalist Christians, who believe that all of the words in the Bible are literal truth, therefore reject the theory of evolution, and many feel that the teaching of evolution in public schools is an affront to their deeply held religious beliefs.

The evolution/creation debate made national headlines in 1925. In that year, Tennessee passed a law banning the teaching of "any theory that denies the story of the Divine Creation of man as taught in the Bible, and [teaching] instead that man has descended from a lower order of animals." At the time, the state-approved biology texts contained information about evolution, and a young schoolteacher named John T. Scopes had taught from that text. Although it is unclear whether any teacher would have been prosecuted otherwise, Scopes agreed to stand trial for his beliefs and arranged with local prosecutors to put him on trial.

The trial attracted national attention as former presidential candidate and noted speaker William Jennings Bryan joined the prosecution team; famous attorney Clarence Darrow joined the defense. With reporters and curious onlookers crowding the courtroom, the trial spilled out onto the courthouse lawn. After a trial marked by grandiose speeches, Scopes was eventually convicted and fined $100, although an appeals court later threw out his conviction. Rather than resolving the debate, the "Scopes Monkey Trial" fueled a controversy that continues today.

- **Why did the Scopes trial attract so much attention in 1925?**

In recent years, opponents of evolution have focused their efforts on discrediting the theory not through religious doctrine, but by developing opposing scientific theories. These scientific theories are often called "creation science," or "intelligent design," implying that a scientific explanation for life on Earth is impossible without the involvement of an intelligent designer, whether or not this designer is the Judeo-Christian God. Although many have mocked supporters of these doctrines, a growing number of doctoral programs in the sciences are beginning to study and report upon these theories.

Creation science and intelligent design are valid alternatives to evolution.

In December of 2002, the Ohio State Board of Education adopted new standards for the teaching of science in the state. Among the new standards was a provision calling for the teaching of scientific theories about origins of the human race other than evolution. Under the standards, students in the state should be able to:

> Describe how scientists continue to investigate and critically analyze aspects of evolutionary theory. (The intent of this indicator does not mandate the teaching or testing of intelligent design.)[1]

For supporters of creation science and intelligent design, the policy was hailed as a victory, even though the standards specifically noted that schools were not required to teach intelligent design. The significance was that the standards opened the debate about evolution, which, after all, is a theory and not a law. Unlike a law, which is able to universally predict results (for example, the law of gravity, which predicts that objects fall toward the earth), a theory is an explanation for an observed set of facts. Although the facts (such as fossilized remains) may be proven, the theory of evolution that many scientists have used to explain the existence of these fossilized remains has not been proven scientifically.

- **Other than evolution, what controversial subjects are taught in public schools?**

Proponents of creation science and intelligent design feel that their own theories do a better job of explaining the current complexity and variety of life forms, as well as fossil records, than does the theory of evolution. According to the Intelligent Design Network, the science of intelligent design is very similar to other sciences that attempt to develop theories to explain observable phenomena:

> These analyses use the same sorts of design detection methods that are used in other sciences such as archaeology, cryptanalysis, forensic sciences, and the search for extra-terrestrial intelligence (SETI).[2]

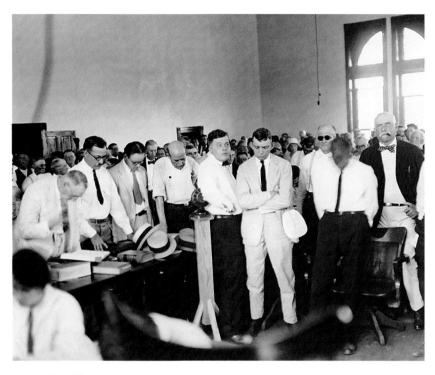

In this telling photograph from the Scopes trial, taken on the morning of July 15, 1925, the court session opens with a prayer. Scopes's attorneys objected to this practice, but the judge allowed it — indicating a possible bias in a case that hinged on the doctrine of separation of church and state. William Jennings Bryan can be seen, head bowed, directly behind the microphone.

According to the group, what makes intelligent design a science is that it has a specific set of criteria that is used to determine whether or not a particular phenomenon is the result of intelligent design. These are: (1) that there is a design that has significance or a message, such as the coded components of DNA molecules, which convey genetic information; (2) that there is no adequate explanation (such as gravity or magnetic forces) that explain the design; and (3) that the design is so complex that it could not have resulted by chance—as they believe is the case with DNA molecules containing thousands of atoms. The group believes that intelligent design (ID) is a better theory than evolution for explaining the complex messages coded in DNA:

> Until a natural law is discovered that can explain this . . . characteristic, ID is the best explanation for the biological information contained in the genetic sequence needed to specify life. In addition, the prospects of the discovery of such a law are bleak since laws produce regularity, not the irregularity absolutely required in DNA.[3]

Efforts to teach creation science are motivated by scientific inquiry, not religion.

Although much of the opposition to teaching evolution might at one time have been strictly based in religion, many supporters of "creation science" and "intelligent design" theory are not necessarily opposed to teaching evolution. In fact, the Supreme Court ruled in *Epperson* v. *Arkansas*[4] (1968) that states could not ban the teaching of evolution outright. Rather, many supporters of creation science and intelligent design are opposed to the teaching of "evolution only."

Although the Supreme Court in 1987 struck down a Louisiana law requiring the teaching of creation science whenever evolution was taught, its decision rested largely on legislative history indicating that the law's sponsor was motivated by religious beliefs rather than increasing academic freedom. However, the Court acknowledged that a law that expanded academic freedom by allowing the "'teaching all of the evidence' with respect to the origin of human beings"[5] might indeed be valid.

> • **Should legislators' motivations in writing laws be used to determine whether those laws are valid? What if the legislators have more than one motivation?**

Walt Brown is one of many people who believe that scientific evidence, rather than religion, is responsible for leading a growing number of scientists to believe in an act of creation (similar to that described in the Bible) and a global flood (similar to the one that Noah survived, according to the Bible). His textbook *In the Beginning: Compelling Evidence for Creation and the Flood* presents in detail "observable, natural phenomena that others can check."[6] As examples of the complexities of life on Earth, he cites examples such as the adult human brain, which has more than 100 trillion electrical connections, and the development of language in humans; to Brown, the only reasonable scientific explanation for such complexities is the involvement of a creator or designer. He cites the lack of fossil evidence of partially developed species, i.e., those with

THE LETTER OF THE LAW

The Tennessee Law Under Which John Scopes Was Tried

AN ACT prohibiting the teaching of the Evolution Theory in all the Universities, Normals and all other public schools of Tennessee, which are supported in whole or in part by the public school funds of the State, and to provide penalties for the violations thereof.

Section 1. *Be it enacted by the General Assembly of the State of Tennessee,* That it shall be unlawful for any teacher in any of the Universities, Normals and all other public schools of the State which are supported in whole or in part by the public school funds of the State, to teach any theory that denies the story of the Divine Creation of man as taught in the Bible, and to teach instead that man has descended from a lower order of animals.

Section 2. *Be it further enacted,* That any teacher found guilty of the violation of this Act, Shall be guilty of a misdemeanor and upon conviction, shall be fined not less than One Hundred ($100.00) Dollars nor more than Five Hundred ($500.00) Dollars for each offense.

—Tennessee Public Acts, Chap. 27 (March 21, 1925)

incomplete organs or limbs, as evidence that each species was created, rather than the result of evolution. Brown also cites evidence that fossilized animals were buried rapidly in deep layers, thereby providing evidence of a global flood.

To Brown, the only plausible scientific explanation for many commonly observed natural phenomena is the involvement of a creator. He believes that it is not creation science but evolution that is motivated by religious belief; many supporters of evolution ignore physically observable evidence of the flood because they want to discredit the Bible. However, the fact that the scientific explanations that he and other creation scientists have developed coincide with biblical beliefs does not invalidate them:

> What is important is not the source of an idea, but whether all evidence supports it better than any other explanation. Science, after all, is a search for truth about how the physical universe behaves. Therefore, let's teach all the science.[7]

> • Is discrediting religious texts such as the Bible one of the goals of modern science? If a scientific theory conflicts with biblical teaching, does that theory count as a competing (religious) belief?

The Intelligent Design Network agrees that teaching evolution has religious implications; its members believe that teaching evolution supports beliefs such as "secular humanism" (believing that right and wrong are determined by individuals and societies) over theistic (believing in divine beings) religions such as Christianity:

> When a public school chooses to discuss with children the question *"Where do we come from?"* the school has chosen to engage in a discussion that unavoidably impacts religion. Metaphorically, it has leaped over the

wall that separates Church from State. Any explanation to this fundamental question will positively or negatively impact religious and nonreligious beliefs. A naturalistic answer to this question negatively impacts theistic religions and supports nonreligions like atheism, agnosticism and secular humanism.[8]

Students can decide for themselves which theory is valid.

In his textbook, Walt Brown advises, "let's teach all the science," which reflects the approach taken by many supporters of creation science and intelligent design. Although the Supreme Court struck down the Louisiana law requiring balanced treatment of evolution and creationism, proponents of creation science and intelligent design have continued to lobby for education standards that teach both evolutionary and creationist theories. They distinguish *Aguillard* by saying that their motivations are scientific, not religious, and that they are not opposed to the teaching of evolution. (The Louisiana law had specified that evolution could not be taught unless creationism was also taught.) Today, proponents seek to have competing theories of natural origins taught side-by-side, with no viewpoint being suppressed. Rather than trying to censor evolution, they are trying to end the scientific establishment's censorship of creation science and intelligent design.

> • **Is suppressing a particular educational subject a form of censorship that violates citizens' freedom of speech?**

In the debate over whether the state of Ohio should include intelligent design in its educational standards, the Intelligent Design Network accused the American Association for the Advancement of Science (AAAS), which had passed a resolution condemning intelligent design, of censoring public debate:

> We believe the office of science and public science education
> is not to indoctrinate students in particular religious or

nonreligious belief systems or world views. Rather the goal of education should be to appropriately educate and inform students so that they will become equipped to make informed decisions about life and the meaning of life. We believe the AAAS resolution and policies are inconsistent with this goal.[9]

Others have criticized the scientific establishment's assumption that evolution is the only possible explanation for the origin of life, and the educational system's adoption of that assumption. Alvin Plantinga writes:

> [T]here is a substantial segment of the population, at least in certain states and certain parts of the country, whose comprehensive beliefs are indeed contradicted by the theory of evolution. . . . Even if their beliefs are irrational from our point of view . . . they have the right to require that public schools not teach as the settled truths beliefs that are incompatible with their comprehensive beliefs.[10]

FROM THE BENCH

May Schools Teach Critiques of Evolution?

From *Edwards* v. *Aguillard*, 482 U.S. 578 (1987):

We do not imply that a legislature could never require that scientific critiques of prevailing scientific theories be taught. Indeed, the Court acknowledged in *Stone* that its decision . . . forbidding the posting of the Ten Commandments did not mean that no use could ever be made of the Ten Commandments, or that the Ten Commandments played an exclusively religious role in the history of Western Civilization. . . . In a similar way, teaching a variety of scientific theories about the origins of humankind to schoolchildren might be validly done with the clear secular intent of enhancing the effectiveness of science instruction. But because the primary purpose of the [Louisiana] Creationism Act is to endorse a particular religious doctrine, the Act furthers religion in violation of the Establishment Clause.

Rather than teaching evolution as incontrovertible truth, many believe that the solution to the problem is to allow students to hear evidence on both sides and to decide—perhaps with the help of their parents—which theory is most plausible. In advocating such an approach, Nel Noddings writes:

> In considering how to treat fundamentalism with genuine respect for its adherents and firm consistency in light of our commitment to intelligence [I believe that] it is not intelligent to censor or proscribe full discussion of any view passionately held by one or more participant[s]. To approach questions about our origins intelligently, we should tell the full story as nearly as we can. All cultures have creation stories, and telling them or encouraging students to find and tell them presents a wonderful opportunity for multicultural education.[11]

- **Would teaching evolution but allowing students to "opt out" work as a compromise?**

Despite failed efforts to limit the teaching of evolution and to teach biblical creation instead, a growing movement of people advocates the teaching of "creation science" or "intelligent design." Supporters say that these theories are scientifically valid, and suppressing them in favor of evolution amounts to academic censorship. They say that the theories are based in sound scientific methods, not religious belief.

Schools Should Treat Evolution as Definitive

The recent events in Ohio are evidence that the forces behind creation science and intelligent design are continuing to make inroads into American education. Despite several Supreme Court rulings invalidating laws that mandated the teaching of creationism or restricted the teaching of evolution, efforts have continued. The controversy in Ohio followed on the heels of a similar controversy in 1999 in Kansas, during which the state board of education released standards that de-emphasized certain aspects of evolution and geology, while encouraging criticism of current scientific beliefs.

Many scientists and concerned citizens believe that "equal time" and criticisms of evolution are not supportive of academic freedom for teachers or academic inquiry by students. Rather, they view these efforts as purely motivated by religious beliefs; even though not everyone shares these religious beliefs, every child's scientific education suffers when evolution is attacked.

Attacks on evolution are misleading.

Although most creationists criticize evolution based on its inconsistency with the biblical account of creation found in the Book of Genesis, leading critics of evolution have developed means of attacking evolution that are not overtly religious, in efforts to lend credibility to their criticisms, especially among people who do not share their fundamentalist religious views. One of the most common criticisms is that evolution is "just a theory" and has not been proven. Polls indicate that creationists have succeeded in creating doubt in the minds of the public:

> Education has a large impact on whether or not one believes [that] the Theory of Evolution is "far from being proven." Over half of Americans without a college degree say Evolution is far from being proven, while half or more of those with a college degree say it is close to being proven. . . . [Einstein's] Theory of Relativity, as a point of comparison, appears to have much more support.[1]

• **Should schools refrain from teaching scientific theories? How would that affect students' academic progress?**

Many scientists have expressed frustration with the "just a theory" criticism. Evolution is not "just a theory," they claim; it is a widely studied theory that has earned a great deal of scientific support after years of careful research. The common meaning of the term "theory," which implies guesswork, is not really consistent with the scientific definition of a theory. In scientific terminology, a "hypothesis" is more akin to a guess, while a "theory" is the result of careful study and analysis. In a study about creationist strategies for influencing public opinion, the People for the American Way Foundation reports:

> Like evolution, gravitational theory, atomic theory, plate tectonics, Copernican theory, geological theory of rock

formation, and Einstein's theory of relativity are all theories based on massive bodies of evidence. All are subject to modification in light of new scientific evidence.

While requiring a physics teacher to teach gravitational theory as "just a theory" is patently absurd, this is precisely how creationists hope to weaken support for evolution. In Alabama . . . a disclaimer [in] all biology textbooks . . . describes evolution as "a controversial theory some scientists present as a scientific explanation for the origin of living

The Ohio Legislature Considers Requiring Critical Analysis of Origins

From a proposed bill:

. . . It is the intent of the general assembly that to enhance the effectiveness of science education and to promote academic freedom and the neutrality of state government with respect to teachings that touch religious and nonreligious beliefs, it is necessary and desirable that "origins science," which seeks to explain the origins of life and its diversity, be conducted and taught objectively and without religious, naturalistic, or philosophic bias or assumption. To further this intent, the instructional program provided by any school district or educational service center shall do all of the following:

(A) Encourage the presentation of scientific evidence regarding the origins of life and its diversity objectively and without religious, naturalistic, or philosophic bias or assumption;

(B) Require that whenever explanations regarding the origins of life are presented, appropriate explanation and disclosure shall be provided regarding the historical nature of origins science and the use of any material assumption which may have provided a basis for the explanation being presented;

(C) Encourage the development of curriculum that will help students think critically, understand the full range of scientific views that exist regarding the origins of life, and understand why origins science may generate controversy.

—H.B. 481, 124th Ohio General Assembly (2001–2002)

things. . . . No one was present when life first appeared on earth. Therefore, any statement about life's origins should be considered as theory, not fact."[2]

In response to efforts to influence public schools to teach intelligent design, the American Association for the Advancement of Science has responded: "The contemporary theory of biological evolution is one of the most robust products of scientific inquiry. It is the foundation for research in many areas of biology as well as an essential element of science education."[3]

Creation science and intelligent design are religious beliefs, not science.

From its beginnings, the creation science movement has faced rejection by the mainstream scientific establishment. According to People for the American Way Foundation:

> The Creation Research Society (CRS), one of America's oldest creationist groups, was founded in Michigan in 1963. Established to circumvent a problem common to its founders—namely, their inability to be published in established, peer-reviewed scientific journals—CRS' primary function is to publish creationist research in its *Creation Research Society Quarterly.*[4]

The Supreme Court has struck down efforts to require the teaching of creation science, on the basis that it is a religious doctrine, rather than a scientific study, declaring: "The tenets of creation science parallel the Genesis story of creation, and this is a religious belief."[5] Yet, the creation science movement has continued its efforts "to claim the power [of] modern science on [its] side," according to James Durham in his study of the effects on religious conservatism on Texas public schools. According to Durham, the theory gained some degree of acceptance due to religious fervor, and "[c]reation science also appealed to many Texans who had not been sufficiently exposed to real science."[6]

> • If a scientist seeks a theory to explain the biblical account of creation, does his or her religious motivation render the process invalid?

FROM THE BENCH

The Supreme Court's Position on Creation Science

From *Edwards* v. *Aguillard*, 482 U.S. 578 (1987):

The question for decision is whether Louisiana's "Balanced Treatment for Creation-Science and Evolution-Science in Public School Instruction" Act (Creationism Act) ... is facially invalid as violative of the Establishment Clause of the First Amendment....

The Creationism Act forbids the teaching of the theory of evolution in public schools unless accompanied by instruction in "creation science." ... No school is required to teach evolution or creation science. If either is taught, however, the other must also be taught.... The theories of evolution and creation science are statutorily defined as "the scientific evidences for [creation or evolution] and inferences from those scientific evidences." ...

The District Court ... held that there can be no valid secular reason for prohibiting the teaching of evolution, a theory historically opposed by some religious denominations. The court further concluded that "the teaching of 'creation-science' and 'creationism,' as contemplated by the statute, involves teaching 'tailored to the principles' of a particular religious sect or group of sects." ... The District Court therefore held that the Creationism Act violated the Establishment Clause either because it prohibited the teaching of evolution or because it required the teaching of creation science with the purpose of advancing a particular religious doctrine.

The Court of Appeals affirmed.... The court observed that the statute's avowed purpose of protecting academic freedom was inconsistent with requiring, upon risk of sanction, the teaching of creation science whenever evolution is taught.... The court found that the Louisiana Legislature's actual intent was "to discredit evolution by counterbalancing its teaching at every turn with the teaching of creationism, a religious belief." ... Because the Creationism Act was thus a law

Many believe that the effort to portray creationism as a science is disingenuous. Robert Pennock writes:

"Creation-science," "abrupt appearance theory," "intelligent design theory," and so on are the creationists' cuckoo eggs that they hope will pass unnoticed, enabling them to garner the

furthering a particular religious belief, the Court of Appeals held that the Act violated the Establishment Clause....We ... now affirm....

The Court has been particularly vigilant in monitoring compliance with the Establishment Clause in elementary and ... secondary schools. Families entrust public schools with the education of their children, but condition their trust on the understanding that the classroom will not purposely be used to advance religious views that may conflict with the private beliefs of the student and his or her family. Students in such institutions are impressionable and their attendance is involuntary....

It is clear from the legislative history that the purpose of the legislative sponsor, Senator Bill Keith, was to narrow the science curriculum. During the legislative hearings, Senator Keith stated:"My preference would be that neither [creationism nor evolution] be taught."... Such a ban on teaching does not promote—indeed, it undermines—the provision of a comprehensive scientific education.

The legislative history documents that the Act's primary purpose was to change the science curriculum of public schools in order to provide persuasive advantage to a particular religious doctrine that rejects the factual basis of evolution in its entirety. The sponsor of the Creationism Act, Senator Keith, explained during the legislative hearings that his disdain for the theory of evolution resulted from the support that evolution supplied to views contrary to his own religious beliefs. According to Senator Keith, the theory of evolution was consonant with the "cardinal principle[s] of religious humanism, secular humanism, theological liberalism, aetheistism [sic]." ...The state senator repeatedly stated that scientific evidence supporting his religious views should be included in the public school curriculum to redress the fact that the theory of evolution incidentally coincided with what he characterized as religious beliefs antithetical to his own....The legislation therefore sought to alter the science curriculum to reflect endorsement of a religious view that is antagonistic to the theory of evolution.

resources (and cultural prestige) of science and the forum of
the science classroom for their own religious ends.[7]

In court, and while talking to school boards, creation
scientists speak of their field as a science rather than a religious
belief. However, a message from the president of the Institute for
Creation Research, John D. Morris, Ph.D., indicates just how
religious the motivations of creationists are:

> Our passion . . . is to see science return to its rightful God-
> glorifying position, and see creation recognized as a strength
> by the body of Christ; supporting Scripture, answering
> questions, satisfying doubts and removing road blocks to
> the Gospel. The . . . Graduate School exists to train students
> in scientific research and teaching skills, preparing effective
> warriors for the faith.[8]

> • **To what degree should students be encouraged to question
> the scientific beliefs that are accepted today?**

Although creationists frequently portray efforts to teach
evolution as thwarting the will of the people—a populace
whom they assert supports religious education—the reality
is that a majority of Americans regard evolution as a valid
scientific concept, while regarding creationism as a religious
belief. The results of a nationwide survey conducted by the
People for the American Way Foundation in November of
1999 indicate:

> The overwhelming majority of Americans (83%) want Evolution
> taught in public schools. While many Americans also support
> the in-school discussion of religious explanations of human
> origins, the majority do not want these religious explanations
> presented as "science". They would like these Creationist ideas
> to be taught about in separate classes other than science

(such as Philosophy) or taught as a "belief". Only a minority of the public (fewer than 3 in 10) wants Creationism taught as science in public schools.[9]

> • **Should national opinions affect what is taught at a local level? How might being "shielded" from particular subjects affect a student's later education?**

At the heart of science are developing explanations based on observable phenomena. However, many supporters of creation science are guided more by their reading of the Book of Genesis than they are by centuries of scientific discoveries. For example, People for the American Way Foundation criticized the involvement of Tom Willis in the development of Kansas' science education standards in 1999:

> Willis, a "Young Earth" creationist, cites Genesis as the authority for his contention that the world was created just 6,000 years ago. . . . Willis also asserts that, contrary to popular belief, dinosaurs lived into the 20th century and were even documented in the 1800s by U.S. government employees. . . .[10]

After the resulting standards required eighth-grade students to "show the weaknesses in the reasoning that led to the hypothesis" regarding the extinction of dinosaurs, the American Association for the Advancement of Science (AAAS) blasted the Kansas standards:

> Besides the fact that the levels of analysis expected by this benchmark are not appropriate for eighth grade students, the wording of this specific example ("show the weaknesses in the reasoning that led to the hypothesis") represents at least an implicit attempt by the Kansas State Board of Education to undermine a currently accepted body of knowledge. In fact, data gathered and analyzed by scientists

from many disciplines lend increasing weight to the pre-vailing scientific ideas about how dinosaurs became extinct. Also, by specifically stating that the hypothesis is weak, the statement contradicts the goal of the standard and the benchmark that seeks to have students develop the ability to analyze evidence.[11]

Ultimately, the position of AAAS, one of the nation's largest scientific societies, was vindicated when Kansas removed the objected-to language in 2001. Evidence suggests that the vast majority of scientists view creation science and intelligent design theories as religious beliefs rather than science. During the debate over the proposed science standards in Ohio, University of Cincinnati political science professor James Bishop conducted a survey of doctoral-level scientists in the state, to which he received responses from approximately one-third of "faculty in four-year, public and private colleges and universities in Ohio for the following fields: astronomy, biology, chemistry, geology, physics, and other natural sciences." According to a press release issued by the university:

Not unexpectedly, those who have the academic training and expertise (PhDs) to teach the basic natural and physical sciences in Ohio's public and private universities regarded the concept of "intelligent design" as an unscientific notion. More than 9 out of 10 (91%) thought it was primarily a religious view. The vast majority (93%) of science profes-sors said they were not aware of "any scientifically valid evidence or an alternate scientific theory that challenges the fundamental principles of the theory of evolution." Only a tiny percentage of them (7%) thought that "intelli-gent design" was either "strongly" or "partly" supported by scientific evidence. Most (90%) believed there was no scientific evidence at all for the idea of "intelligent design".

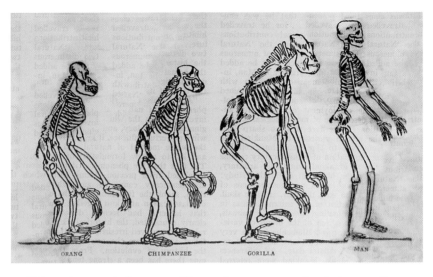

This early twentieth-century illustration compares the skeletons of vertebrates to illustrate Charles Darwin's theory of the evolution of humans. In fact, humans are not believed to be descended from orangutans, chimpanzees, or gorillas; rather, they are believed to share common ancestors with all three species. The idea of humankind's being descended from any kind of "ape" offends more conservative religious thinkers—and was a source of humor in the nineteenth century—but some have found compromise in creation science and intelligent design.

And 3% were "not sure". Furthermore, when asked if they ever used the ID concept in their research, virtually all of them (97%) said "no." [12]

Students should be taught the truth, not forced to figure it out for themselves.

A frequent argument made by creationists is that all voices should be heard—that local schools should have the opportunity to teach competing theories, and that students should have the right to decide for themselves what to believe. However, this approach has been criticized on several grounds. Many fear that local schools in some places will be dominated by religious fundamentalists, who will encourage schools to provide misinformation to students. The students, they fear, will lack the maturity and insight to separate truth from dogma. As a result, suggests People for the American Way Foundation, in areas dominated by religious viewpoints, students will lack the scientific knowledge necessary to pursue higher education or enter scientific fields:

> Real education requires accurate information and free inquiry. Otherwise the recent experience of one Texas teacher will be replayed in classrooms across the country. This teacher says: "[Her students believe] that men have one less rib than women, and that the science textbooks are inaccurate in their portrayals of human skeletons. . . ."[13]

> • **How capable are high school students of deciding which scientific principles are valid and which are invalid?**

Another criticism is that students simply lack the maturity to make decisions for themselves, and therefore it is not fair to teach widely accepted theories such as evolution alongside controversial theories such as creation science and intelligent design.

Others believe that students can only be taught so much and that it is a waste of valuable time to teach creation science and intelligent design. Willard Young writes:

> Schools and teachers have a responsibility to their students to give them, in the limited time available, the best education possible. To meet that responsibility they must expose their students to the most reliable knowledge of the day, and make them aware of the important intellectual, scientific, and other accomplishments of our time. They must avoid the danger of misleading and confusing students by mixing questionable or erroneous material with that of high confidence.[14]

- **How important are scientific educational standards today? What is the relationship in the rest of the world between religion and science? Between religion and education?**

Perhaps most important to the case against creationism is the overwhelming belief within the scientific community that evolution is a valid and important concept, while creationism theories are not valid subjects for study. In his survey of doctoral-level scientists in the state of Ohio, Professor Bishop discovered that most of the scientists thought that it was important to teach evolution but thought that intelligent design theory should *not* be taught:

> Ohio's science professors felt just as strongly about what should or should not be taught about the controversy in Ohio schools. Most all of them (92%) thought "Ohio high school students should be tested on their understanding of the basic principles of the theory of evolution in order to graduate." When asked, however, if such students should also be tested on their knowledge of the concept of "intelligent design" in order to graduate, most of them (90%) said "no." [15]

Scientists and concerned parents have fought efforts to have creation science and intelligent design taught in schools. They believe that evolution is an important and sound scientific concept, whereas creationist approaches are based in religion rather than science. Most importantly, they believe that teaching these alternative theories diminishes the quality of students' education.

A Look to
the Future

The terrorist attacks of September 11, 2001, rekindled the smoldering debate over religion in public schools. To some, the post-9/11 era was a time for widespread prayer and reflection, and school prayer was a natural reaction needed for the nation to heal. However, others felt that the animosity many felt toward people of the Islamic faith was further evidence that this nation needs to learn religious tolerance, and that school prayer would only have an isolating effect on members of minority religions.

> • **What do the terrorist attacks of September 11, 2001, mean for the American government? For democracy in general?**

As the twenty-first century began, many wondered what the future would hold. Some have felt that advances in technology have—now more than ever—created a need for religious and moral instruction of all children. The availability of almost unlimited content on the Internet is a concern for many parents. With claims that human cloning is taking place, many believe that the nation needs to return to traditional values, and that religious instruction could play a pivotal role. To many people, however, restoring school prayer would reverse decades of progress in creating a diverse society.

Teaching the Bible

Although religion has not been entirely removed from public schools, it has been largely relegated to voluntary student clubs meeting outside of class time. To many, the removal of religion from classroom instruction has left a void, not just from a religious standpoint, but also from an educational standpoint. It is difficult to deny that the Bible and Christian religion have been extremely influential in the development of American culture and government, and many people would like to see the Bible taught in public schools.

The movement to teach about the Bible in public schools is gaining momentum nationwide, despite the Supreme Court's ruling over four decades ago that daily reading of Bible verses is unconstitutional. Supporters of a "Bible curriculum" say that the Bible is an important part of civilization and history, and therefore it should be studied in an academic manner. According to People for the American Way Foundation, which has opposed such curricula, "It is perfectly acceptable to teach about the Bible in public schools, so long as the instruction is presented objectively, as part of secular education, and not as history or from a particular sectarian perspective."[1] Yet, this organization questions whether curricula being adopted in Florida, Louisiana, Tennessee, and elsewhere are truly objective, and it has been involved in several lawsuits challenging Bible curricula.

The Supreme Court has not ruled directly on the matter. Although the Court suggested in *Stone* v. *Graham*, "[T]he

This display of the Ten Commandments outside a public high school in Ohio was one of several issues challenged by the American Civil Liberties Union (ACLU) between 1999 and 2002. Between 1997 and 1999, the monument stood alone, but other monuments to Anglo-American legal documents were added after the ACLU's lawsuit; this made the religious display part of a larger cultural display and complicated the suit. A federal court ruled the display unconstitutional in June, and an appeals court upheld the ruling in November. Religious groups are currently lobbying Congress to allow states to decide whether such displays are permissible.

Bible may constitutionally be used in an appropriate study of history, civilization, ethics, comparative religion, or the like,"[2] the Court in that case struck down a Kentucky law requiring that the Ten Commandments be posted in each public school classroom. Despite the influence of the Ten Commandments on American law, the Court held that their posting on classroom walls had a plainly religious—and therefore unconstitutional— purpose. The constitutionality of Bible curricula will ultimately be determined by school systems' motivation for adopting the curricula. Perhaps the defining question is whether a curriculum contains any criticisms of the truth and validity of biblical teachings, or whether the Bible is taught as both truth and good policy.

Supreme Court Trends

In contrast to the Supreme Court headed by Chief Justice Earl Warren during the 1960s—the Court that struck down the practice of school prayer—today's Court, headed by Chief Justice William Rehnquist, is much more politically conservative. Although the Court has steadfastly maintained a position against organized school prayer—for example, invalidating prayer at high school football games in the 2000 *Santa Fe Independent School District* v. *Doe*[3] decision—the Court has, at the same time, allowed for greater involvement of religious groups in public schools. A significant example is *Good News Club* v. *Milford Central School*[4] (2001), which allowed parents to hold after-school religious meetings for elementary school students. The Court may not have torn down the wall of separation between church and state, but the wall is certainly lower now than it was before the Court took its conservative turn.

A landmark Supreme Court decision that did not directly involve religion in public schools is nevertheless important to note because it might have a significant, though indirect, effect. In *Zelman* v. *Simmons-Harris* (2002),[5] the Court upheld an

Ohio "voucher" program, which provides yearly scholarships to students living in the Cleveland city school district, thereby enabling the students to attend the school of their choice, including religious schools. The program was open to any student in the district and did not specify which schools

The U.S. Department of Education's Position on Religion in Public Schools

From the Department of Education's "Guidance on Constitutionally Protected Prayer in Public Elementary and Secondary Schools":

The relationship between religion and government in the United States is governed by the First Amendment to the Constitution, which both prevents the government from establishing religion and protects privately initiated religious expression and activities from government interference and discrimination. The First Amendment thus establishes certain limits on the conduct of public school officials as it relates to religious activity, including prayer....

The Supreme Court has repeatedly held that the First Amendment requires public school officials to be neutral in their treatment of religion, showing neither favoritism toward nor hostility against religious expression such as prayer. Accordingly, the First Amendment forbids religious activity that is sponsored by the government but protects religious activity that is initiated by private individuals, and the line between government-sponsored and privately initiated religious expression is vital to a proper understanding of the First Amendment's scope. As the Court has explained in several cases, "there is a crucial difference between government speech endorsing religion, which the Establishment Clause forbids, and private speech endorsing religion, which the Free Speech and Free Exercise Clauses protect."

The Supreme Court's decisions over the past forty years set forth principles that distinguish impermissible governmental religious speech from the constitutionally protected private religious speech of students. For example, teachers and other public school officials may not lead their classes in prayer, devotional readings from the Bible, or other religious activities. Nor may school officials attempt to persuade or compel students to participate in prayer or other religious the students could attend, so long as the school met state educational standards. The Court held:

> [W]here a government aid program is neutral with respect to religion, and provides assistance directly to a broad class

activities. Such conduct is "attributable to the State" and thus violates the Establishment Clause.

Similarly, public school officials may not themselves decide that prayer should be included in school-sponsored events.…Nor may school officials grant religious speakers preferential access to public audiences, or otherwise select public speakers on a basis that favors religious speech.…

Although the Constitution forbids public school officials from directing or favoring prayer, students do not "shed their constitutional rights to freedom of speech or expression at the schoolhouse gate," and the Supreme Court has made clear that "private religious speech, far from being a First Amendment orphan, is as fully protected under the Free Speech Clause as secular private expression." Moreover, not all religious speech that takes place in the public schools or at school-sponsored events is governmental speech. For example, "nothing in the Constitution . . . prohibits any public school student from voluntarily praying at any time before, during, or after the school day," and students may pray with fellow students during the school day on the same terms and conditions that they may engage in other conversation or speech. Likewise, local school authorities possess substantial discretion to impose rules of order and pedagogical restrictions on student activities, but they may not structure or administer such rules to discriminate against student prayer or religious speech. For instance, where schools permit student expression on the basis of genuinely neutral criteria and students retain primary control over the content of their expression, the speech of students who choose to express themselves through religious means such as prayer is not attributable to the state and therefore may not be restricted because of its religious content. Student remarks are not attributable to the state simply because they are delivered in a public setting or to a public audience. As the Supreme Court has explained: "The proposition that schools do not endorse everything they fail to censor is not complicated," and the Constitution mandates neutrality rather than hostility toward privately initiated religious expression.

of citizens who, in turn, direct government aid to religious schools wholly as a result of their own genuine and independent private choice, the program is not readily subject to challenge under the Establishment Clause. A program that shares these features permits government aid to reach religious institutions only by way of the deliberate choices of numerous individual recipients. The incidental advancement of a religious mission, or the perceived endorsement of a religious message, is reasonably attributable to the individual recipient, not to the government, whose role ends with the disbursement of benefits.[6]

In effect, the Court upheld a program in which public funds would be distributed to private religious schools on the principle that the funds were distributed indirectly through the students and their parents.

> • **Should the Bible be taught in public schools? Should the teaching of other texts, such as the Koran, be required wherever the Bible is taught? What would count as a "religious text," and who would decide which religions were taught?**

It is difficult to predict what effect the decision upholding school vouchers will have on the influence of religion in public schools. On the one hand, the decision itself signals the Court's increased acceptance of the use of public funding for religious education, and perhaps students, parents, and school systems will be more likely to test the limits of the law by increasing the role of religion in the public schools. On the other hand, because voucher programs make attending private religious schools more financially feasible, perhaps religiously devout students and their parents will become more likely to attend private schools and less interested in infusing religion into the public schools. Whatever happens, because Americans are both deeply religious and diverse, the influence of religion in public schools will always remain controversial.

As the twenty-first century begins, the controversy over religion in public schools continues. Two major issues are teaching about the Bible in public schools, and the potential exodus of students from public school systems as voucher programs become more widespread.

Religion in Public Schools: Historical Roots and Current Controversies

1 Richard C. McMillan, *Religion in the Public Schools: An Introduction*, Mercer University Press, 1984.
2 *Zorach* v. *Clauson*, 343 U.S. 306 (1952).
3 George DeWan, "School Prayer Divides LI," in *Long Island: Our Story*, available online at www.lihistory.com.
4 Madalyn Murray O'Hair, *An Atheist Epic: Bill Murray, the Bible, and the Baltimore Board of Education*, American Atheist Press, 1970.
5 *Engel* v. *Vitale*, 370 U.S. 421 (1962).
6 *Abington School Dist.* v. *Schempp*, 374 U.S. 203 (1963).
7 *Lemon* v. *Kurtzman*, 403 U.S. 602 (1971).
8 *Lee* v. *Weisman*, 505 U.S. 577 (1992).
9 *Santa Fe Independent School District* v. *Doe*, No. 99–62 (June 19, 2000).
10 Peter J. Ferrara, *Religion and the Constitution: A Reinterpretation*, Free Congress Research & Education Foundation, 1983.

Point: Prayer Should Be Allowed to Return to Public Schools

1 *Engel* v. *Vitale*, 370 U.S. 421 (1962).
2 *Engel* v. *Vitale*, 370 U.S. 421 (1962) (Stewart, J., dissenting).
3 *Engel* v. *Vitale*, 370 U.S. 421 (1962).
4 Robert H. Bork, *The Tempting of America*, Touchstone, 1990, pp. 16, 69.
5 Ibid., p. 95.
6 *Abington School Dist.* v. *Schempp*, 374 U.S. 203 (1963).
7 George DeWan, "School Prayer Divides LI," in *Long Island: Our Story*, available online at www.lihistory.com.
8 Americans United for Separation of Church and State, "People and Events," *Church & State* (July/August 2002).
9 David Barton, "Ten Steps to Change America," available online at www.wallbuilders.com/resources/search/detail.php?ResourceID=64.
10 *Lee* v. *Weisman*, 505 U.S. 577 (1992) (Scalia, J., dissenting).
11 Dalia Sussman, "America Wants God in the Pledge," ABCNews.com (July 1, 2002), available online at abcnews.go.com/sections/us/DailyNews/pledge_poll0207 01.html.

12 Eric Tiansay, "Students Defy Ruling Barring Invocation by Praying," Charisma News Service (June 3, 2002).
13 Dalia Sussman, "Public Backs School Prayer," ABCNews.com (June 19, 2002), available online at abcnews.go.com/sections/us/DailyNews/poll000328.html.
14 *Lee* v. *Weisman*, 505 U.S. 577 (1992) (Scalia, J., dissenting).
15 Cong. Rec. H3006 (May 7, 1998) (statement of Rep. Istook).

Counterpoint: Prayer Does Not Belong in Public Classrooms

1 Religious Liberty and the Bill of Rights, Hearing Before the Subcomm. on the Constitution of the House Comm. on the Judiciary (July 10, 1995) (statement of Lisa Herdahl).
2 Charles A. Rohn, "Plenty of Religious Expression in Public Schools," *The School Administrator* (Web Edition, June 2000).
3 People for the American Way Foundation, "Back to School with the Religious Right" (August 28, 2002), available online at www.pfaw.org/pfaw/general/default.aspx?oId=3634.
4 *Santa Fe Independent School District* v. *Doe*, No. 99–62 (June 19, 2000).
5 *Lee* v. *Weisman*, 505 U.S. 577 (1992).
6 *Herdahl* v. *Pontotoc County School District*, 933 F. Supp. 582 (N.D. Miss. 1996).
7 Rob Boston, "David Barton: Master of Myth and Misinformation," *Freedom Writer* (June 1996).
8 *Herdahl* v. *Pontotoc County School District*, 933 F. Supp. 582 (N.D. Miss. 1996).
9 Religious Liberty and the Bill of Rights, Hearing Before the Subcomm. on the Constitution of the House Comm. on the Judiciary (July 10, 1995) (statement of Lisa Herdahl).
10 *Abington School District* v. *Schempp*, 374 U.S. 203 (1963).

Point: Religious Clubs in Public Schools Should Be Treated More Fairly

1 *Widmar* v. *Vincent*, 454 U.S. 263 (1981).
2 20 U.S.C. §§4071–4074.

100

3 20 U.S.C. §§4071.

4 *Board of Education of Westside Community Schools* v. *Mergens*, 496 U.S. 226 (1990).

5 *Good News Club* v. *Milford Central School*, No. 99–2036 (June 11, 2001).

6 Ontario Consultants on Religious Tolerance, "The Federal Equal Access Act: Student-Led Clubs in Public High Schools," available online at www.religioustolerance.org/equ_acce.htm.

7 Jeff Donaldson, "Schools Will Allow Distribution of Religious Material," *The Desert Sun* (Palm Springs, California) (August 22, 2001).

8 The Liberty Counsel, news release, August 9, 2001.

9 20 U.S.C. §4072.

10 *Ceniceros* v. *Board of Trustees of San Diego Unified School District*, 106 F.3d 878 (9th Cir. 1997).

11 *Prince* v. *Jacoby*, No. 99–35490 (September 9, 2002).

12 Peter J. Ferrara, *Religion and the Constitution: A Reinterpretation*, Free Congress Research & Education Foundation, 1983.

13 *Board of Education of Westside Community Schools* v. *Mergens*, 496 U.S. 226 (1990).

14 *Good News Club* v. *Milford Central School*, No. 99–2036 (June 11, 2001).

15 Anti-Defamation League, "Religion in Public Schools: Student Religious Clubs," available online at www.adl.org/religion_ps/clubs.asp.

16 Brief for the States of Alabama, Iowa, Louisiana, Mississippi, Nebraska, Ohio, South Carolina, Tennessee, Texas, Utah, and Virginia in *Good News Club* v. *Milford Central School*, No. 99–2036 (June 11, 2001).

Counterpoint: Religious Clubs in Public Schools Have Unfair Advantages

1 Ellen Johnson, *Atheists' Rights and Religious Expression in the Public Schools* (introduction), American Atheists, 2000, p. 6.

2 Ibid., p. 5.

3 20 U.S.C. §§4071–4074.

4 Ellen Johnson, *Atheists' Rights and Religious Expression in the Public Schools* (introduction), American Atheists, 2000, p. 7.

5 Ken Camp, "Students Asked to Start Campus Groups," *The Baptist Standard* (July 24, 2000).

6 20 U.S.C. §4071.

7 The Coaching Center, "Involving Adults in Ministry," available online at www.gocampus.org/alliance/impact/impact1-3-2.htm.

8 Fun with Faith Clubs, "How to Start Your Own Traditional Club," available online at www.funwithfaith.com/howto.htm.

9 *Ceniceros* v. *Board of Trustees of San Diego Unified School District*, 106 F.3d 878 (9th Cir. 1997) (Lay, J., dissenting).

10 20 U.S.C. §4072.

11 *Ceniceros* v. *Board of Trustees of San Diego Unified School District*, 106 F.3d 878 (9th Cir. 1997) (Lay, J., dissenting).

12 Teens 4 Jesus Youth Ministries, "Campus Outreach Ideas," available online at www.teens4jesus.org/resources/clubs/resources/outreach.htm.

13 *Herdahl* v. *Pontotoc County School District*, 933 F. Supp. 582 (N.D. Miss. 1996).

14 20 U.S.C. §4071.

15 *Prince* v. *Bethel School District*, No. 99–35490 (9th Cir. September 9, 2002).

16 See www.thearda.com/RCMS/2000/State/49.htm. The U.S. Census is prohibited from collecting and reporting data about religious affiliation.

17 *Herdahl* v. *Pontotoc County School District*, 933 F. Supp. 582 (N.D. Miss. 1996).

18 Anti-Defamation League, "Student Religious Clubs," available online at www.adl.org/religion_ps/clubs.asp.

19 *Ceniceros* v. *Board of Trustees of San Diego Unified School District*, 106 F.3d 878 (9th Cir. 1997) (Lay, J., dissenting).

20 The Coaching Center, "Involving Adults in Ministry," available online at www.gocampus.org/alliance/impact/impact1-3-2.htm.

21 Ellen Johnson, introduction to *Atheists' Rights and Religious Expression in the Public Schools*, American Atheists, 2000, p. 6.

Point: Schools Should Teach Theories Other Than Evolution

1 State Board of Education of Ohio, "Academic Content Standards: Science" (December 10, 2002).

2 Intelligent Design Network, "Response to the Resolution of the American Association for the Advancement of Science that Seeks to Censor Intelligent Design" (December 16, 2002), available online at www.intelligentdesignnetwork.org.

3 Ibid.

4 *Epperson* v. *Arkansas*, 393 U.S. 97 (1968).

5 *Edwards* v. *Aguillard*, 482 U.S. 578 (1987).

6 Walt Brown, *In the Beginning: Compelling Evidence for Creation and the Flood*, 17th ed., Center for Scientific Creation, 2001, p. 228.

7 Ibid.

8 Intelligent Design Network, "Response to the Resolution of the American Association for the Advancement of Science That Seeks to Censor Intelligent Design" (December 16, 2002), available online at www.intelligentdesignnetwork.org.

9 Ibid.

10 Alvin Plantinga, "A Modest Proposal," in *Intelligent Design Creationism and Its Critics*, ed. Robert T. Pennock, MIT Press, 2001, p. 783.

11 Nel Noddings, *Educating for Intelligent Belief or Unbelief*, Teachers College Press, 1993, p. 143.

Counterpoint: Schools Should Treat Evolution as Definitive

1 People for the American Way Foundation, *Evolution and Creationism in Public Education: In-Depth Reading of Public Opinion*, March 2000, p. 42.

2 People for the American Way Foundation, *Sabotaging Science: Creationist Strategies in the '90s* (November 1999), pp. 11–12, citing "Creationism Fight Returns to Nation's Classrooms," *The New York Times* (March 9, 1996).

3 American Association for the Advancement of Science, "AAAS Board Resolution on Intelligent Design Theory" (October 18, 2002), available online through www.aaas.org.

4 People for the American Way Foundation, *Sabotaging Science: Creationist Strategies in the '90s* (November 1999), p. 16.

5 *Edwards* v. *Aguillard*, 482 U.S. 578 (1987).

6 James R. Durham: *Secular Darkness: Religious Right Involvement in Texas Public Education, 1963–1989*, Peter Lang, 1995, p. 72.

7 Robert T. Pennock, "Why Creationism Should Not Be Taught in the Public Schools," in *Intelligent Design Creationism and Its Critics*, ed. Robert T. Pennock, MIT Press, 2001.

8 See www.icr.org/abouticr/intro.htm.

9 People for the American Way Foundation, *Evolution and Creationism in Public Education: An In-Depth Reading of Public Opinion* (March 2000), p. 5.

10 People for the American Way Foundation, *Sabotaging Science: Creationist Strategies in the '90s* (November 1999), p. 3.

11 Joint Statement from the National Research Council, American Association for the Advancement of Science, and the National Science Teachers Association Regarding the Kansas Science Education Standards (September 23, 1999), available online through www.aaas.org.

12 University of Cincinnati, press release, "Majority of Ohio Science Professors and Public Agree: 'Intelligent Design' Mostly About Religion" (October 11, 2002).

13 People for the American Way Foundation, *Sabotaging Science: Creationist Strategies in the '90s* (November 1999), 17.

14 Willard Young, *Fallacies of Creationism*, Detselig Enterprises, 1985.

15 University of Cincinnati, press release, "Majority of Ohio Science Professors and Public Agree: 'Intelligent Design' Mostly About Religion" (October 11, 2002).

A Look to the Future

1 People for the American Way Foundation, *Back to School with the Religious Right* (August 28, 2002).

2 *Stone* v. *Graham*, 449 U.S. 39 (1980) (*per curiam*).

3 *Santa Fe Independent School District* v. *Doe*, No. 99–62 (June 19, 2000).

4 *Good News Club* v. *Milford Central School*, No. 99–2036 (June 11, 2001).

5 *Zelman* v. *Simmons-Harris*, No. 00–1751 (June 27, 2002).

6 Ibid.

In February of 2003, U.S. Secretary of Education Rod Paige released a guiding statement on constitutionally protected prayer in public elementary and secondary schools. This document, an excellent source of information and a powerful directive for all publicly funded American schools, can be found online at www.ed.gov/inits/religionandschools/prayer_guidance.html.

In Favor of Religion in Public Schools/Alternatives to Evolution

Barton, David. *America: To Pray or Not to Pray?: A Statistical Look at What Happened When Religious Principles Were Separated from Public Affairs*, 6th ed. WallBuilder Press, 1991.

Bork, Robert H. *The Tempting of America.* Touchstone, 1990.

Brown, Walt. *In the Beginning: Compelling Evidence for Creation and the Flood*, 7th ed. Center for Scientific Creation, 2001.

Ferrara, Peter J., *Religion and the Constitution: A Reinterpretation.* Free Congress Research & Education Foundation, 1983.

Noddings, Nel. *Educating for Intelligent Belief or Unbelief.* Teachers College Press, 1993.

The American Center for Law and Justice
www.aclj.org
Legal organization founded by Pat Robertson, supporting religious expression in schools.

The Coaching Center
www.gocampus.org
Provides information and support to students wishing to start Christian clubs in schools.

Fun With Faith Clubs
www.funwithfaith.com
Helps Christian parents start religious clubs for elementary school students.

The Liberty Counsel
www.lc.org
Legal organization litigating on behalf of individual religious expression.

The Intelligent Design Network
www.intelligentdesignnetwork.org
Advocates for the teaching of intelligent design in public schools. Information about intelligent design and reasons for including it in curricula.

The Rutherford Institute
www.rutherford.org
A conservative legal group supporting free exercise of religion and the rights of abortion protesters, among other issues.

Teens 4 Jesus Ministries

www.teens4jesus.org

Offers advice to students who wish to start Christian clubs in schools.

Against Coercive Religious Practices in Public Schools/ Alternatives to Evolution

Detwiler, Fritz. *Standing on the Premises of God: The Christian Right's Fight to Redefine America's Public Schools.* New York University Press, 1999.

Durham, James R. *Secular Darkness: Religious Right Involvement in Texas Public Education, 1963–1989.* Peter Lange, 1995.

Murray O'Hair, Madalyn. *An Atheist Epic: Bill Murray, the Bible, and the Baltimore Board of Education.* American Atheist Press, 1970.

Pennock, Robert T., ed. *Intelligent Design Creationism and Its Critics.* MIT Press, 2001.

Young, Willard. *Fallacies of Creationism.* Detselig Enterprises, 1985.

American Atheists

www.atheists.org

Supports the rights of atheists to be free from public expressions of religion.

The American Civil Liberties Union

www.aclu.org

Organization supporting a wide range of civil liberties, including abortion, criminal justice, and free speech as well as separation of church and state.

Americans United for Separation of Church and State

www.au.org

Stresses the importance of church–state separation to religious liberty.

The Anti-Defamation League

www.adl.org

Fights anti-Semitism and other forms of religious discrimination.

People for the American Way

www.pfaw.org

Dedicated to protecting religious freedom, safeguarding public education, and combating the influence of religious dogma in public affairs. Site offers in-depth reports about religion and creationism in public schools.

Legislation and Case Law

Zorach v. *Clauson*, 343 U.S. 306 (1952)
Held that public schools may release students during the school day for off-campus religious instruction.

Engel v. *Vitale*, 370 U.S. 421 (1962)
Held that requiring students to recite a prayer composed by the state's Board of Regents violates the Constitution's establishment clause.

Abington School Dist. v. *Schempp*, 374 U.S. 203 (1963) and *Murray* v. *Curlett*, 374 U.S. 203 (1963)
Decided simultaneously; ruled that daily Bible readings and recitation of the Lord's Prayer violated the establishment clause.

Epperson v. *Arkansas*, 393 U.S. 97 (1968)
State law prohibiting the teaching of evolution violates the establishment clause.

Stone v. *Graham*, 449 U.S. 39 (1980) (*per curiam*)
State law requiring that Ten Commandments be posted in public school classrooms violates the establishment clause.

Widmar v. *Vincent*, 454 U.S. 263 (1981)
Freedom of Speech prevents universities from discriminating against religious clubs.

The Equal Access Act, 20 U.S.C. §§4071−4074
Requires high schools to give "equal access" to religious clubs before and after actual classroom instruction.

Edwards v. *Aguillard*, 482 U.S. 578 (1987)
State law requiring creation science to be taught whenever evolution was taught violated the establishment clause.

Westside Community Bd. of Ed. v. *Mergens*, 496 U.S. 226 (1990)
The Equal Access Act is constitutional and requires high schools to allow Bible clubs if they allow groups such as chess clubs to meet.

Lee v. *Weisman*, 505 U.S. 577 (1992)
Allowing a rabbi to lead a prayer at a public high school graduation violates the establishment clause.

Herdahl v. *Pontotoc County School District*, 933 F. Supp. 582 (N.D. Miss. 1996)
School violated the establishment clause by allowing a religious club to lead prayers over the school intercom.

Ceniceros v. *Board of Trustees of San Diego Unified School District*, 106 F.3d 878 (9th Cir. 1997)
The Equal Access Act prohibits discriminating against religious clubs' activities during lunchtime.

Santa Fe Indep. Sch. Dist. v. *Doe*, No. 99−62 (June 19, 2000)
Leading prayers over the public address system at a high school football game violates the Constitution.

Good News Club v. *Milford Central School*, No. 99–2036 (June 11, 2001)
  Freedom of speech requires that elementary schools allow parents to lead after-school religious club on same basis as other clubs are allowed to operate.

Newdow v. *United States*, No. 00–16423 (9th Cir. June 26, 2002)
  In a decision that was not implemented, an appeals court ruled that the phrase "under God" rendered the Pledge of Allegiance unconstitutional.

Zelman v. *Simmons-Harris*, No. 00–1751 (June 27, 2002)
  Cleveland school district can provide monetary support ("vouchers") allowing students to attend schools of their own choice, including religious schools.

Prince v. *Jacoby*, No. 99–35490 (9th Cir. September 9, 2002)
  Freedom of speech requires school to allow religious clubs access to school resources, such as audio-visual equipment and vehicles.

Concepts and Standards

the free exercise clause
the establishment clause
separation of church and state
the Lemon test
legislating politics from the bench
voluntary, student-initiated prayer
secular purpose
opting out
equal access
the free speech clause
open forum
no-discrimination doctrine
endorsement
noninstructional time
evolution
creation science
intelligent design
scientific theory
scientific hypothesis
scientific law
Bible curricula
school vouchers

Beginning Legal Research

The goal of POINT/COUNTERPOINT is not only to provide the reader with an introduction to a controversial issue affecting society, but also to encourage the reader to explore the issue more fully. This appendix, then, is meant to serve as a guide to the reader in researching the current state of the law as well as exploring some of the public-policy arguments as to why existing laws should be changed or new laws are needed.

Like many types of research, legal research has become much faster and more accessible with the invention of the Internet. This appendix discusses some of the best starting points, but of course "surfing the Net" will uncover endless additional sources of information—some more reliable than others. Some important sources of law are not yet available on the Internet, but these can generally be found at the larger public and university libraries. Librarians usually are happy to point patrons in the right direction.

The most important source of law in the United States is the Constitution. Originally enacted in 1787, the Constitution outlines the structure of our federal government and sets limits on the types of laws that the federal government and state governments can pass. Through the centuries, a number of amendments have been added to or changed in the Constitution, most notably the first ten amendments, known collectively as the Bill of Rights, which guarantee important civil liberties. Each state also has its own constitution, many of which are similar to the U.S. Constitution. It is important to be familiar with the U.S. Constitution because so many of our laws are affected by its requirements. State constitutions often provide protections of individual rights that are even stronger than those set forth in the U.S. Constitution.

Within the guidelines of the U.S. Constitution, Congress—both the House of Representatives and the Senate—passes bills that are either vetoed or signed into law by the President. After the passage of the law, it becomes part of the United States Code, which is the official compilation of federal laws. The state legislatures use a similar process, in which bills become law when signed by the state's governor. Each state has its own official set of laws, some of which are published by the state and some of which are published by commercial publishers. The U.S. Code and the state codes are an important source of legal research; generally, legislators make efforts to make the language of the law as clear as possible.

However, reading the text of a federal or state law generally provides only part of the picture. In the American system of government, after the legislature passes laws and the executive (U.S. President or state governor) signs them, it is up to the judicial branch of the government, the court system, to interpret the laws and decide whether they violate any provision of the Constitution. At the state level, each state's supreme court has the ultimate authority in determining what a law means and whether or not it violates the state constitution. However, the federal courts—headed by the U.S. Supreme Court—can review state laws and court decisions to determine whether they violate federal laws or the U.S. Constitution. For example, a state court may find that a particular criminal law is valid under the state's constitution, but a federal court may then review the state court's decision and determine that the law is invalid under the U.S. Constitution.

It is important, then, to read court decisions when doing legal research. The Constitution uses language that is intentionally very general—for example, prohibiting "unreasonable searches and seizures" by the police—and court cases often provide more guidance. For example, the U.S. Supreme Court's 2001 decision in *Kyllo* v. *United States* held that scanning the outside of a person's house using a heat sensor to determine whether the person is growing marijuana is unreasonable—*if* it is done without a search warrant secured from a judge. Supreme Court decisions provide the most definitive explanation of the law of the land, and it is therefore important to include these in research. Often, when the Supreme Court has not decided a case on a particular issue, a decision by a federal appeals court or a state supreme court can provide guidance; but just as laws and constitutions can vary from state to state, so can federal courts be split on a particular interpretation of federal law or the U.S. Constitution. For example, federal appeals courts in Louisiana and California may reach opposite conclusions in similar cases.

Lawyers and courts refer to statutes and court decisions through a formal system of citations. Use of these citations reveals which court made the decision (or which legislature passed the statute) and when and enables the reader to locate the statute or court case quickly in a law library. For example, the legendary Supreme Court case *Brown* v. *Board of Education* has the legal citation 347 U.S. 483 (1954). At a law library, this 1954 decision can be found on page 483 of volume 347 of the U.S. Reports, the official collection of the Supreme Court's decisions. Citations can also be helpful in locating court cases on the Internet.

Understanding the current state of the law leads only to a partial understanding of the issues covered by the POINT/COUNTERPOINT series. For a fuller understanding of the issues, it is necessary to look at public-policy arguments that the current state of the law is not adequately addressing the issue. Many groups lobby for new legislation or changes to existing legislation; the National Rifle Association (NRA), for example, lobbies Congress and the state legislatures constantly to make existing gun control laws less restrictive and not to pass additional laws. The NRA and other groups dedicated to various causes might also intervene in pending court cases: a group such as Planned Parenthood might file a brief *amicus curiae* (as "a friend of the court")—called an "amicus brief"—in a lawsuit that could affect abortion rights. Interest groups also use the media to influence public opinion, issuing press releases and frequently appearing in interviews on news programs and talk shows. The books in POINT/COUNTERPOINT list some of the interest groups that are active in the issue at hand, but in each case there are countless other groups working at the local, state, and national levels. It is important to read everything with a critical eye, for sometimes interest groups present information in a way that can be read only to their advantage. The informed reader must always look for bias.

Finding sources of legal information on the Internet is relatively simple thanks to "portal" sites such as FindLaw (*www.findlaw.com*), which provides access to a variety of constitutions, statutes, court opinions, law review articles, news articles, and other resources—including all Supreme Court decisions issued since 1893. Other useful sources of information include the U.S. Government Printing Office (*www.gpo.gov*), which contains a complete copy of the U.S. Code, and the Library of Congress's THOMAS system (*thomas.loc.gov*), which offers access to bills pending before Congress as well as recently passed laws. Of course, the Internet changes every second of every day, so it is best to do some independent searching. Most cases, studies, and opinions that are cited or referred to in public debate can be found online— and *everything* can be found in one library or another.

The Internet can provide a basic understanding of most important legal issues, but not all sources can be found there. To find some documents it is necessary to visit the law library of a university or a public law library; some cities have public law libraries, and many library systems keep legal documents at the main branch. On the following page are some common citation forms.

COMMON CITATION FORMS

Source of Law	Sample Citation	Notes
U.S. Supreme Court	*Employment Division* v. *Smith*, 485 U.S. 660 (1988)	The U.S. Reports is the official record of Supreme Court decisions. There is also an unofficial Supreme Court ("S.Ct.") reporter.
U.S. Court of Appeals	*United States* v. *Lambert*, 695 F.2d 536 (11th Cir.1983)	Appellate cases appear in the Federal Reporter, designated by "F." The 11th Circuit has jurisdiction in Alabama, Florida, and Georgia.
U.S. District Court	*Carillon Importers, Ltd.* v. *Frank Pesce Group, Inc.*, 913 F.Supp. 1559 (S.D.Fla.1996)	Federal trial-level decisions are reported in the Federal Supplement ("F.Supp."). Some states have multiple federal districts; this case originated in the Southern District of Florida.
U.S. Code	Thomas Jefferson Commemoration Commission Act, 36 U.S.C., §149 (2002)	Sometimes the popular names of legislation—names with which the public may be familiar—are included with the U.S. Code citation.
State Supreme Court	*Sterling* v. *Cupp*, 290 Ore. 611, 614, 625 P.2d 123, 126 (1981)	The Oregon Supreme Court decision is reported in both the state's reporter and the Pacific regional reporter.
State statute	Pennsylvania Abortion Control Act of 1982, 18 Pa. Cons. Stat. 3203-3220 (1990)	States use many different citation formats for their statutes.

115

page:

13: Associated Press, AP

18: © CORBIS

22: © Bettmann/CORBIS

40: Associated Press, AP/Steve Yeater

55: Associated Press, The Garden City Telegram/Graham K. Johnson

63: Associated Press, AP/ Bruce Newman

73: © Underwood & Underwood/ CORBIS

89: © Bettmann/CORBIS

94: Associated Press, AP/David Kohl

ALAN MARZILLI, of Durham, North Carolina, is an independent consultant working on several ongoing projects for state and federal government agencies and nonprofit organizations. He has spoken about mental health issues in more than 20 states, the District of Columbia, and Puerto Rico; his work includes training mental health administrators, nonprofit management and staff, and people with mental illness and their family members on a wide variety of topics, including effective advocacy, community-based mental health services, and housing. He has written several handbooks and training curricula that are used nationally. He managed statewide and national mental health advocacy programs and worked for several public interest lobbying organizations in Washington, D.C. while studying law at Georgetown University.